# ABOUT THE AUTHOR

Dr Peter McCue is a retired clinical psychologist with a longstanding interest in anomalous phenomena. He has personally investigated many cases, as well as writing numerous articles on paranormal and UFO-related matters, and being interviewed for radio, Internet, and television. He is the author of three previous books: *Zones of Strangeness: An Examination of Paranormal and UFO Hot Spots* (AuthorHouse, 2012); *Paranormal Encounters on Britain's Roads: Phantom Figures, UFOs and Missing Time* (The History Press, 2018); *Britain's Paranormal Forests: Encounters in the Woods* (The History Press, 2019).

# CURSES, COINCIDENCES & MALIGN INFLUENCE

A Parapsychological Perspective

by

Peter A. McCue

Published 2021 by Abramis academic publishing

www.abramis.co.uk

ISBN 978 1 84549 794 1

© Peter A. McCue 2021

All rights reserved

This book is copyright. Subject to statutory exception and to provisions of relevant collective licensing agreements, no part of this publication may be reproduced, stored in a retrieval system, or transmitted in any form or by any means, without the prior written permission of the author.

Typeset in Garamond

This book is sold subject to the conditions that it shall not, by way of trade or otherwise, be lent, re-sold, hired out, or otherwise circulated without the publisher's prior consent in any form of binding or cover other than that which it is published and without a similar condition including this condition being imposed on the subsequent purchaser.

Abramis is an imprint of arima publishing.

arima publishing
ASK House, Northgate Avenue
Bury St Edmunds, Suffolk IP32 6BB
t: (+44) 01284 700321

www.arimapublishing.com

# CONTENTS

*Acknowledgements* ............................................................................ 1
*Foreword by Ron Halliday* ................................................................ 3
*Preface* ............................................................................................... 7
1. Introduction ................................................................................. 9
2. Strange Coincidences ................................................................ 19
3. The Paranormal ........................................................................ 29
4. Paranormal Vendettas .............................................................. 55
5. Cursed Objects and Materials .................................................. 73
6. Cursed by Black-Eyed Children ............................................. 113
7. Family Curses .......................................................................... 127
8. Curses in the Music and Film Industries ............................. 139
9. Reflections and Speculations ................................................. 157
*Notes* .............................................................................................. 165
*Bibliography* .................................................................................. 175
*Index* .............................................................................................. 179

# ACKNOWLEDGEMENTS

I should like to thank the following: Ron Halliday, for kindly writing the foreword to this book; David T. Muir, for his help with proofreading; Jonathan Beecher of White Crow Books, for permission to quote passages from the late Mary Rose Barrington's book *Talking about Psychical Research*; Patrick Huyghe of Anomalist Books, for permission to quote from Barrington's book *JOTT*; Chris Salewicz, for permission to quote from his book *Jimmy Page*; Dr Mario Varvoglis and the Parapsychological Association, for permission to quote from an online article by him; Andy Dixon, Content Editor with Highland News & Media Ltd, for permission to reproduce the text of an article that appeared in *Highland News*; the University of London Library at Senate House, for permission to quote from a book by the late Harry Price; Darren Ritson and Michael Hallowell, for providing information about cases they've investigated; Catriona Malan, for drawing my attention to the case of 'Flight 191'; Robert McLuhan, for providing contact details regarding Mario Varvoglis.

# FOREWORD

Are some individuals prone to 'bad luck' or deliberately targeted by an evil force? Or are incidents of this genre simply another form of myth? It's a fascinating subject, which Peter McCue discusses with enthusiasm and erudition. The author covers a range of events linked to 'curses, coincidences and malign influence' from an 'evidential and parapsychological perspective'. There is, as it transpires, a wealth of fascinating cases, covering a variety of phenomena, which McCue discusses and comments on objectively. He neither rejects nor accepts the events related, but offers a reasoned critique, allowing the reader to make a balanced judgement on the validity of each case.

Is it possible that cursing someone can actually have a malign effect on that person? If someone falls ill after the enactment of a curse – for example, the pressing of pins into a wax doll representing the intended victim – is that evidence of its reality, or is it pure coincidence? How reliable are claims by people that they have been cursed and that bad luck has followed them as a consequence? Each case must be judged on its merits, but as McCue points out, apparent coincidences can result from ignoring contrary evidence.

Take, for example, claims that with John Lennon of the Beatles, the number 9 was significant in his life; or that flights numbered 191 are particularly prone to accidents. In the case of Lennon, by focusing on selected facts, it might seem that the number 9 played a significant role in his life. But what if we subconsciously ignore facts that point in a different direction – numbers in Lennon's life that undermine the alleged significance of the number 9? For example, he died aged 40, not 39. Do we select points that back up a connection and ignore negative evidence because we, as human beings, need to create a world where science is unable to answer every question in our lives? There are more quite fascinating coincidences that McCue considers, and which raise questions about the nature of fortuity in people's lives.

On the matter of cursing people, if we believe that wishing something evil produces an effect, then we should identify how the 'curse' affects the intended target. Can we identify a vector? McCue draws attention to terms significant in parapsychology, such as *telepathy* and *psychokinesis*, whereby a connection is effected between individuals or between an individual and an object, without an obvious transmitter. These concepts, however, remain controversial within mainstream science.

A fascinating aspect of the book is the spread of cases that McCue considers. In the chapter on 'Paranormal Vendettas', for example, he looks at the case of 'The Drummer of Tedworth' in the seventeenth century. Moving on to more recent times, he examines alleged 'misfortune befalling UFO researchers', which demonstrates that the concept of 'paranormal vendettas' is a continuing phenomenon with a long history. No doubt, with more information, it would be possible to look at instances considerably further back in time.

Are some objects capable of emitting 'negative energy'? There's a widespread belief that certain objects can ward off evil influences – such as a horseshoe or a rowan tree – and that others bring good luck – for example, a rabbit's foot or a four-leafed clover. So it's not difficult to envisage the inverse. According to tradition, a horseshoe hung the 'wrong' way up can induce bad forces rather than provide protection. McCue again considers a variety of cases, assessing the evidence as to whether there is any validity to claims that the object in question has exercised a negative influence. Best known are claims over the opening of Tutankhamun's tomb and the various deaths that followed. Again, are we connecting up dots to form a picture that doesn't exist in reality?

Probably the strangest cases that McCue discusses relate to curses by 'black-eyed children'. These are instances where people encounter 'children or child-like entities with totally black eyes or with black cavities where the eyes should be'. Before reading McCue's accounts, I was unaware of the extent of this phenomenon, which, as he suggests, may result from a 'trickster intelligence' bringing about 'theatrical paranormal displays'. It's a fascinating concept, but one has to ask *why* the manifestations are being orchestrated. Anyone who has investigated poltergeist cases will concur with the idea that irrespective of what sort of intelligence is behind the manifestations, the phenomena themselves often appear to be pointless displays of paranormal activity. Is the same true of black-eyed children?

However, we're on more familiar ground with McCue's discussion of 'family curses' – the notion that certain families are the victims of a disproportionate amount of bad luck. The Kennedy family is certainly one where, through various generations, it is said that they have experienced more than their fair share of misfortune – John F. Kennedy was infamously assassinated in Dallas, his older brother Joe was killed in a plane accident during World War II, his younger brother Robert was also assassinated, and Edward Kennedy's reputation was forever besmirched by events at Chappaquiddick and the death of Mary Joe Kopechne in 1969. Bad luck dogged various other members of the Kennedy clan – for example, the death of John Kennedy Jr in a plane crash in 1999. On the face of it, these events appear to make a case for a 'family curse'. McCue reviews them and points out that, taken in isolation, each 'misfortune' may be explained in a rather more prosaic way. In this context, there are also interesting discussions of the Romanov Dynasty of Russia and the Grimaldi family of Monaco.

Certain areas of activity attract speculation, and the film and music industries have generated more than their fair share of conspiracy theories. One that I'm familiar with is the number of artists who have died in various plane or car accidents – Otis Redding, John Denver, Buddy Holly, and Eddie Cochrane are a few names that spring to mind. Otis Redding features in another speculative group – artists who have died at the age of 27. Brian Jones of the Rolling Stones and Amy Winehouse can be added to the list. However, there are many more musicians and actors who were neither killed in accidents nor died aged 27, so is this another instance of the human mind looking for connections that don't exist? But what makes this book such a fascinating read is the possibility that there *might* be an indefinable *something* playing with our world.

McCue's final chapter, an analysis of the evidence, is a masterly summing up and worth reading on its own. He suggests various explanations and neither dismisses nor accepts that the different cases presented require a paranormal explanation. This, in my opinion, is how we must judge the 'curse' in all its various forms. It's difficult to pin down evidence to confirm its reality. It remains a somewhat nebulous phenomenon. Even so, there's enough evidence to suggest that for all its ephemeral nature, something odd and inexplicable is, in certain cases, taking place. I can thoroughly recommend this book.

*Ron Halliday,*
*Bridge of Allan,*
*September 2021*

# PREFACE

When strange things happen to people, or when they experience bad luck, they may come to believe that they've been cursed. Even if they don't come to this conclusion themselves, others may infer that a curse is operating. This book looks at curses or alleged curses from an evidential and parapsychological perspective. That is, the focus is on whether some assumed curses are 'real' and, if so, how they work. As such, this is not a history of witchcraft.

I've referenced print sources using what's known as the 'Harvard system', which is tidier than using endnotes, since one can go straight from the reference to the bibliography to get the full publication details. For Internet sources, I have used endnotes. However, I've been selective in referencing Internet items. Those I've listed are likely to be more useful to readers than some of those that I looked at in passing.

By the time the book is published, some of the referenced Internet items may no longer be available via the addresses given, although by using a search engine such as Google, it may be possible to find the material elsewhere on the Internet.

I've occasionally used endnotes to append supplementary information that might have been distracting if it had appeared in the main text.

Regarding witnesses with whom I've had personal contact, I've made it clear whether the names given are real or pseudonymous. However, in respect of the names cited by other authors, the situation isn't always clear, since writers don't always say when they're using pseudonyms. But where I'm aware that a pseudonym has been used, I've indicated that.

In Chapter 7, which deals with supposed family curses, I've given just the family name in the index. For example, I've referred to 'The Kennedy family', instead of indexing the name of every Kennedy mentioned.

The photographs displayed in this book were all taken by me. They're mainly from Scotland. That's not because of any bias against locations elsewhere. It simply reflects the fact that I'm based in Scotland and it's easier for me to visit places relatively close to my home.

# CHAPTER 1

# INTRODUCTION

This is a book about curses, strange coincidences, and the role that 'dark forces' may play in our lives, or – at least – in the lives of some people. I'll be citing numerous cases; and in the final chapter, I'll try to draw some conclusions, although there are many uncertainties, and often grounds for doubt and scepticism.

Inevitably, I've alluded to the past, but I've made no attempt to provide a comprehensive history of witchcraft – my focus has generally been on the present or recent past. And, as the subtitle indicates, I'm looking at the subject of curses from a parapsychological perspective. There's a good reason for doing so, because if some curses are 'real', they clearly involve paranormal phenomena.

Our lives are punctuated with events, good and bad, that affect our well-being. In many cases, these happenings are the result of our own actions. For example, people who pursue careers in boxing, football, or rugby may increase their risk of early-onset dementia, through incurring recurrent bangs to the head. And people who engage in 'base jumping' (making parachute jumps from cliffs, bridges, skyscrapers, and the like) will be at a higher risk of dying early than people who pursue less hazardous recreations.

Leaving aside unhappy outcomes directly attributable to our actions or genetic make-up, there are also events that we put down to chance or bad luck, such as being run over by a drunk driver, being struck by lightning, or being killed in an unexpected terrorist incident. We tend to think that falling victim to such things is largely a random matter – being in the wrong place at the wrong time. But when people experience a seemingly disproportionate amount of bad luck, they may look in other directions and infer that they've been singled out or cursed. That was certainly the case a few centuries ago in the British Isles, when a belief in witchcraft was commonplace.

## TERMINOLOGY

The word 'curse' is ambiguous. Used as a *verb*, it refers to *making an utterance or engaging in some activity (maybe symbolic) aimed at harming someone or something by paranormal means*. I'll refer to such behaviour as a *cursing ritual*. Used in this sense, the words 'curse' and 'cursed' don't necessarily imply success ('I cursed her, but it didn't work'). When 'curse' is used as a *noun* (a naming word), it may simply be shorthand for a cursing ritual ('The curse didn't work'). Alternatively, it could be used to mean that the target of a curse did indeed suffer misfortune. For example, if we hear of a curse on a particular family, the implication is that they've experienced difficulties. Of course, whether their problems have been brought about by evil intentions or a cursing ritual might be debatable. Furthermore, when people, such as journalists, refer to 'curses' in connection with recurrent bad luck, they may be using the expression figuratively rather than literally.

Imagine that Jill hates Grace and wishes her bad luck, and that Grace then becomes ill and dies. Imagine, further, that Jill confides in a friend that although she hated Grace, she didn't actually perform any mental or physical ritual to hasten her death. Does that mean that Jill *didn't* curse Grace? Obviously, this comes down to how we define cursing. It may be that negative thoughts and feelings can affect others, even if there's no explicit cursing ritual (see the section on 'dark thoughts', below).

There are numerous terms with more or less identical meanings relating to magical practices. I prefer the word 'paranormal' to 'magical', since the latter is a bit vague, with connotations not limited to the notion of invoking hidden forces to bring about desired results. For example, in a cooking competition, a food critic might describe a contestant's dish as 'simply magical', meaning nothing more than 'delightful'.

The expressions 'incantation', 'spell', and 'enchantment' have roughly the same meaning, referring to a set form of words or actions aimed at having a paranormal effect. If this takes a verbal form, the words might be spoken, sung, chanted, or written down, perhaps by someone claiming to possess, or thought to possess, special knowledge and power (e.g. a witch, wizard, sorcerer, or sorceress – again, the terms are pretty much interchangeable). The ability to cast spells has also been attributed to non-human entities, such as fairies. Of course, if spells are intended to harm others, they're likely to be called curses, maledictions, or imprecations. The opposite of a curse is a *benediction* or *blessing*, although these words have a more religious ring than 'curse' or 'malediction'. For instance, if we hear of a priest blessing a house, we're likely to assume that he called on God to protect and bestow peace on its occupants.

In what follows, I'll use the term *instigator* to refer to someone who initiates a curse, and the term *agent* for the intelligence or entity that carries it out. The instigator and agent may or may not be the same. I'll refer to the intended victim of a curse as the *target*. However, in many cases, the existence of a curse is merely an inference, based on a succession of bad luck, without there being a clear indication of who supposedly instigated it. For example, if different generations of a family seem to experience a disproportionate amount of misfortune, it might be inferred that they've been cursed, even if the person or people behind the supposed curse can't be identified. Cases of supposed family curses are discussed in Chapter 7.

Maybe curses don't always require a conscious instigator or agent. It could be that certain actions trip off impersonal processes that bring about trouble or misfortune? There are, for example, reports of ghostly phenomena being precipitated by building renovations (see Chapter 3). Of course, these cases are open to different interpretations; and, as I'll explain in the final chapter, there are problems in construing curses in a purely mechanistic way.

## Types of curse

For clarity, I'd like to distinguish between two types of curse (or assumed curse). The first is what I'll call a *Type I curse*, where the target person or group experiences *disturbing phenomena of a distinctly paranormal character*. A *Type II curse*, on the other hand, results in (or is claimed to result in) the target person or group experiencing *a disproportionate amount of bad luck*.

Imagine that Bob curses Jack and that, very soon after, Jack and his family are plagued by poltergeist phenomena. That's the sort of situation I have in mind regarding Type I curses. Examples are cited in Chapter 4.

In the case of presumed Type II curses, each incident or episode of bad luck – such as your contracting a serious illness, being involved in an accident, your marriage breaking up, or your suffering a major financial setback – might be attributed to purely prosaic factors, the rough and tumble of life. In other words, none of those things, in itself, might seem overtly paranormal. And yet, taken together, a close succession of unhappy events might incline you to believe that a malign intelligence orchestrated them, particularly if you've reason to think that someone who has dabbled in the occult 'has had it in for you'. But if it's *not* known whether anyone had a malign intent and performed a cursing ritual (which is typically the case), it's very speculative to attribute a run of bad luck to a curse. All told, then, when it comes to deciding whether curses really are working in the background, supposed Type II curses throw up more problems than alleged Type I curses.

Some cases may feature both Type 1 and Type II elements. In his book *Cursed Britain*, Thomas Waters (2020, pp. 224-9) mentions John Lundy, a man from Devon, who maintained that he was cursed in 2003 by an acquaintance called George Foster. Foster died three weeks later. But around the same time, Lundy and his wife suffered serious health problems. In late 2004, things started going wrong at Mr and Mrs Lundy's home. For example, light bulbs kept fusing, and the couple heard strange noises at night, coming from the walls. They apparently feared that this was the work of Foster's spirit.

## THE EVIL EYE

In past years, at least, a widespread belief was that people could be cursed simply by being looked at, particularly if the person doing the looking (the one deemed as having the proverbial 'evil eye') happened to be harbouring negative feelings (e.g. envy). For example, a glance from a childless woman at a pregnant woman might have been interpreted as sinister, and if any mishap befell the pregnant woman, the childless woman might have been blamed for transmitting a curse.

Weatherly (2017, p. 176) explains that the Sumerians, Babylonians and Assyrians mentioned the evil eye repeatedly, that the Egyptians feared it, and that the ancient Greeks and Romans took it seriously. He points out that it's mentioned in the Bible (e.g. in Proverbs 23:6 and 28:22). And Weatherly (p. 177) notes that belief in the power of the evil eye has been especially strong in Italy over the years.

INTRODUCTION

## CURSED OBJECTS

We sometimes hear of supposedly cursed objects (dolls, paintings, items of jewellery, etc.). In such cases, the object isn't the target of the curse, but rather the presumed 'carrier' of a malediction, meaning that someone who owns or takes possession of it risks bad luck or disturbing phenomena. I'll mention one instance here and cite numerous further examples in a later chapter.

In February 2021, a couple of reports in the *Brighton Argus* told of a woman from Kent who'd acquired a painting, and who subsequently experienced ghostly phenomena in her flat.[1,2] For example, her television set changed channels by itself, and doors opened and slammed shut. The manifestations ceased almost as soon as she got rid of the picture. Admittedly, that may have been just a coincidence. Interestingly, though, it was suggested that the suspect painting depicted Marie Laveau, a 19th-century practitioner of Vodou (Voodoo). She was born in New Orleans, in Louisiana, but there's uncertainty about the precise year of her birth.[3]

## BLACK MAGIC

By definition, the employment of curses is a part of *black magic* – ritualistic practices aimed at summoning real or supposed magical (paranormal) powers for selfish, harmful and evil purposes.

Arguably, there's a fine line between white magic and black magic. Imagine two scenarios. In the first, Julie is engaged to Dave and is faithful to him. However, a jealous acquaintance of hers spreads a malicious rumour that Julie has been playing around with other men. Dave gets to hear this. Julie pleads with him to realize that the rumour is false, but he doesn't believe her, and he breaks off the engagement. Distraught, she contacts a 'white witch', who casts a spell to make Dave see sense. The spell works, and Julie and Dave are reunited. In the second scenario, Julie is engaged to Dave, but she really is unfaithful to him. This leaks out, and Dave gets to hear about it. He breaks off the engagement. Julie contacts a witch, who casts a spell to make Dave resume the engagement, and the spell works.

Now, in the first scenario, the spell wasn't coercive. It was simply aimed at clearing up a misunderstanding – that is, enabling Dave to see the truth, that his fiancée hadn't betrayed him. In the second scenario, however, the spell could be seen as coercive (since it subverts Dave's will, inducing him to resume a relationship with someone who'd let him down, and who might do so again). Accordingly, one could say that in the first scenario, *white* magic was employed, and in the second case, it was *black* magic.

## Satanism

It's worth making a distinction between black magic and *Satanism*. The former is a broader concept, not necessarily linked with ideas about Satan. In past centuries, 'Satanism' was largely a term of condemnation that Christian groups used in referring to their opponents. For example, after the Reformation, Catholics and Protestants accused each other of Satanism.

According to an article by Joe Carter, three 'major trends' are evident in contemporary Satanism: (1) theistic or religious Satanism, (2) atheistic or philosophical Satanism, and (3) reactive or adolescent Satanism.[4]

*Theistic Satanists* venerate Satan as an actual supernatural deity or 'dark force'. Carter notes that researchers have estimated that the global number of theistic Satanists is very small, in the low thousands.

*Atheistic Satanists* don't acknowledge the existence of God or Satan. Instead, they treat Satan as a symbolic adversary of traditional religion and morality, and as a symbol of the self-gratifying human ego, the real object of their worship. In 1966, Anton Szandor LaVey (1930-97), who was born Howard Stanton Levey, established the Church of Satan in California. His Satanism is of the atheistic type, and he presented it as a type of ethical egoism, not the practice of evil. He urged his followers to be law-abiding and to indulge in pleasure only if it didn't harm others. But despite the atheistic and materialistic slant of his views, he believed that people could exercise magical powers, by intensely imagining their desired goals and directing their willpower towards them.

*Reactive Satanists*, if I've understood the concept correctly, treat Satan as an evil god, as he's viewed in Christianity, but they choose to worship him rather than shun him, this being an act of adolescent rebellion against parents or society more generally. Carter suggests that reactive Satanists may constitute the largest group of modern Satanists. Arguably, though, there's a 'reactive' aspect to atheistic Satanism as well: its use of Satan as a symbol could be seen as a theatrical ploy that's intended to shock and draw attention.

INTRODUCTION

## DANGEROUS EMOTIONS

In everyday speech, the phrase 'scared to death' isn't taken literally. It's generally used to describe situations in which people feel *very* afraid – albeit, perhaps, only briefly. However, it appears to be a fact that sudden strong emotions, such as fear, can occasionally lead to death, particularly with people having pre-existing heart problems.

Our bodies react to perceived threats by activation of what's known as the sympathetic branch of the autonomic nervous system. This so-called 'fight or flight' response entails things such as an increased heart rate and increased sweating. It's mediated by substances known as hormones or 'chemical messengers' (e.g. adrenaline), which are secreted into the bloodstream and quickly travel around the body, having a range of effects, readying the body for action. Generally, this may be conducive to survival, but the high level of these hormones can have negative effects. In the case of the heart, a high level of circulating adrenaline can result in too much calcium going into the organ, which – in turn – can lead to a potentially fatal disruption of the heart rhythm.

Imagine that, unexpectedly, two old friends, Steve and Mick, have a heated argument, and that Steve tells Mick: 'I'm into black magic, and I'm going to put a curse on you. You'll soon be dead!' Let's further assume that Mick has a heart problem and that, whether or not he's taken the threat of the curse seriously, the argument has badly upset him, and that he drops down dead just minutes after the row. One possibility would be that Steve really did curse Mick, and that it 'worked' (i.e. in a paranormal way), or that Steve's angry thoughts killed Mick, without the need of a cursing ritual. On the other hand, it could be that it was Mick's physiological reaction to the row, coupled with his heart problem, that killed him, not a curse.

It appears that long-term stress can compromise the working of the body's immune system, rendering people more prone to infections and perhaps more susceptible to cancer. It follows that if people become chronically anxious, erroneously thinking that they've been cursed, they may be at a greater risk of becoming unwell. If that happens, their illness might be wrongly attributed to a malign influence related to the supposed curse.

## **PREVENTION, CURE, AND EXPLOITATION**

Prevention, it's said, is better than cure. Over the centuries, people have taken all sorts of steps to ward off malign influences. Apotropaic (evil-averting) measures have included, for example, nailing a horseshoe above the door of a house or barn, or concealing 'witchcraft-repelling' items (crossed knives, opened scissors, etc.) about one's home (Waters, 2020, pp. 21-3). Outside the home, people might carry with them, or wear, amulets of one sort or another. For instance, In Scotland, starting around the early 18th century, silver or gold 'luckenbooth brooches' were produced, and supposedly had a protective effect.

One of the many books written by the British occultist Dion Fortune (1890-1946) was *Psychic Self-Defence*.[5] It was first published in 1930. My copy – the one I'll reference – is a 2001 edition, published in the USA with the title *Psychic Self-Defense*. The book discusses 'psychic attacks' and how they might be diagnosed and countered. However, Fortune (p. 227) states that the book isn't a satisfactory handbook for the treatment of 'psychic disorders', but rather a guide to where help might be sought. She was extremely eclectic in her beliefs, embracing all sorts of notions, such as astral travel, astrology, reincarnation, and the protective effect of magical rituals. In modern parlance, her beliefs might be called 'New Age'. But I must confess that I don't find her book very lucid and coherent, and I therefore skipped over much of the content. But I'll briefly mention a few of the things that she says about dealing with psychic attacks (curses).

She contends that much can be done on the 'physical plane' to help a victim. For example, she suggests that sunlight is very helpful, because it strengthens a person's aura, making it much more resistant (p. 169). And she states that anything that improves the person's physical condition (e.g. games, physical training, or massage) can be invaluable, although the victim should certainly avoid solitude (p. 170). As for more specifically 'psychic' measures, she refers to the practice of meditating on abstract qualities, such as peace, protection, and the love of God, to bring about a 'harmonizing' of the emotions and to counteract harmful autosuggestions (p. 193). Another method, which she considers much more effective, is the invocation of 'external potencies', and the use of formal means for focusing their force. This can range from something simple (e.g. a prayer, accompanied by the sign of the cross, calling on Jesus Christ) to elaborate exorcism rituals (pp. 193-5).

People who believe they've been cursed may call on the services of supposed experts to relieve them of the malediction. In Britain in past centuries, these individuals were known by various names, such as *canny-folk, clever-folk, conjurors, cunning-folk, warlocks, wise-women,* and *wizards.* No doubt many of them were, to some extent, confidence tricksters, exploiting people's fears of malign supernatural influence. However, as Waters (2020, pp. 129-38) cogently argues, in many cases, they no doubt performed a useful psychotherapeutic function, by exerting a powerful placebo effect – convincing their clients that they could, and would, become free of supposed curses.

Exploitation of people's fears about curses has persisted into modern times. Waters (*ibid.*, p. 242) cites a particularly bad case, that of a Leicester woman calling herself 'Sister Grace'. In 2006, she was jailed and fined for defrauding clients. One of them, a 53-year-old mother, went to an initial tarot reading session, costing £100. In due course, she was persuaded into giving away her life savings (£20,932) and borrowing £28,000 from a bank. Sister Grace warned that without that money being handed over, a curse would kill the woman's son and husband, and her daughter would never get married.

## DARK THOUGHTS

It's not unusual for people to feel happy when they hear of misfortune or embarrassment befalling people they don't like. The posh name for this (taken from German) is 'schadenfreude', which literally means 'harm joy'.[6] For example, if it comes to light that a well-known MP has become embroiled in a sex scandal, the news might be relished by his or her political opponents.

Most of us probably think of ourselves as decent, well-intentioned people. But on occasions, even the most virtuous of us will probably wish others a degree of bad luck! Take, for instance, sporting events. Imagine, for example, that you're watching Rafael Nadal playing in the final of a major tennis tournament, and that you're a Nadal fan. You'll hope that he aims his shots well, holds his service games, and breaks his opponent's serve. In other words, as well as wanting Nadal to play well, you'll probably be hoping that the other player makes mistakes.

A competitive job interview is another situation where this will occur. Imagine that you're one of several shortlisted candidates for a job that you're very keen to get. Naturally, you'll want to impress the interview panel and perform better than the other candidates. In other words, you'll want them to perform *less well* than you do.

Few of us are saints, and we can probably all name people we don't like. Sometimes, we may have thoughts about them that aren't curses as such, but get rather close. For example, during a moment of frustration or anger with a colleague (let's call him John), we might say, 'As far as I'm concerned, you can go to hell!' Typically, this won't mean, literally, that we want him to be consigned to hell; and if something goes badly wrong in John's life, we'll not attribute it to our negativity. After all, we tend to think that our thoughts and feelings don't affect the material world around us – that if a disliked acquaintance is diagnosed with cancer, for instance, we're in no way to blame. However, as I'll explain in Chapter 3, evidence suggests that some people, at least, can exert a *psychokinetic* ('mind over matter') effect on their environment. Furthermore, as I'll also explain, there's scientific evidence suggesting that *positive* thoughts and intentions regarding other people (the opposite of cursing) can facilitate healing. It goes without saying that if good wishes can benefit people, negative wishes may have a harmful effect.

# CHAPTER 2

# STRANGE COINCIDENCES

When people experience a seemingly disproportionate amount of bad luck, they (or others) may infer that something more than random bad luck or simple coincidence has been at work. In this chapter, I'll cite cases involving strange coincidences and ask whether that's what the incidents were – events simply coming together by chance – or whether something else was involved.

Carl Gustav Jung (1875-1961) trained as a psychiatrist and, for a time, was a close associate of Sigmund Freud (1856-1939), the founder of psychoanalysis. Eventually, the men's views started to diverge, and Jung's version of psychoanalysis became known as 'analytical psychology'. It was Jung who introduced the term 'synchronicity', which he applied to 'meaningful coincidences' between events with no apparent causal connection between them. Such synchronicities, it has been argued, should be distinguished from ordinary coincidences involving nothing more than chance. However, critics of Jung have dubbed his notions as pseudoscientific and unprovable.

In terms of the 'laws of chance', coincidences are to be expected, and we should be wary about making too much of them. Imagine, for instance, that a teacher randomly assigns two schoolgirls to adjacent seats, and that it happens that the girls share the same first name (Susan), the same birthday, and that they're both left-handed. Before inferring that destiny somehow decreed that these left-handed Susans with the same birthday should be seated together, we need to recognize that there'll be very many cases where this *doesn't* happen. When it does, it's likely to attract comment and be remembered; when it doesn't, it will pass without mention or further thought. This highlights what's known as the *confirmation bias* ('cherry-picking'): selecting instances that fit a pattern or pet theory, while ignoring others that don't.

This is a complex matter, and it's not always easy to say whether coincidences of one sort or another reflect pure chance or something more mysterious. The following are some illustrative cases.

## CASE EXAMPLES

### Case 1: The Erdington murders

In a book on unexplained phenomena, Roy Bainton (2013, pp. 566-7) cites an intriguing case from Erdington, which is about five miles from the centre of Birmingham in the Midlands of England. It was the setting for a murder in 1817, and then another in 1974. Bainton states that in both instances, the victim's body was found on 27 May (although according to another source, that's *not* the case[1]). Both victims were reportedly 20-year-old women with the same birthday. In each case, the girl had visited her best friend on the evening of Whit Monday. Each of them had been at a dance on the evening of her murder, and each was wearing a new dress. Both of them had been raped and strangled, and the accused man in each case (both of whom were acquitted) had the surname 'Thornton'!

At first sight, this may seem mind-boggling. But maybe we shouldn't dismiss pure chance and a degree of cherry-picking as explanations for the correspondences. The murders were separated by over 150 years. There were probably other murders in the locality in the intervening years, and most likely they *didn't* follow the aforementioned pattern (e.g. the victims may *not* have been 20-year-old women). Sadly, rape is a relatively common offence; and if a rapist wants to silence his victim, it's perhaps likely that he'll try to strangle her. As for the surname of the above-mentioned suspects, maybe Thornton was, and perhaps still is, a relatively common surname in the area.

### Case 2: John Lennon and the number 9

John Lennon (1940-80), the former Beatle, believed that the number *nine* featured prominently in his life. At first sight, there seems to be some evidence for this. For example, he was born on *9* October 1940; his first home in Liverpool was at *9* Newcastle Road in the Wavertree area of the city; the Beatles were 'discovered' by their manager-to be, Brian Epstein, on *9* November 1961; they played on the Ed Sullivan Show in the USA on *9* February 1964; they broke up after *9* years together; and although Lennon was fatally shot on 8 December 1980 in New York City, it was then *9* December in the UK, where he was born.[2]

Arguably, some of the supposed 'evidence' for a preponderance of nines in Lennon's life smacks of massaging details to fit the theory. For example,

Lennon used to travel to his local art college on a number 72 bus. If the 7 and 2 that make up 72 are added together, we get *9*! Similarly, Lennon and Yoko Ono's first apartment in the Dakota Building in New York City was number 72. So, again: 7+2 = *9*.

I looked up the dates of birth of Lennon's two sons. Julian Lennon was born on 8 April 1963 in Liverpool. Sean Lennon was born on *9* October 1975 in New York City. Therefore, in the case of Sean, there's some support for the 'nine theory', since he was born on the ninth of the relevant month (October). But given that Julian was born on the eighth of the relevant month (April), his birthdate doesn't accord with the theory, unless we grant ourselves the indulgence of adding together the last two digits of the relevant year (1963) to come up with yet another questionable nine!

Lennon was close to an aunt of his known as 'Mimi'. I looked up her details. Her date of birth was 24 April 1906, which doesn't seem to support the 'nine theory'. Neither does the date of her death, 6 December 1991, unless significance is given to the second nine in 1991. The first nine in 1991 doesn't really deserve mention, because a vast swathe of the world's population was born in the 1900s.

## Case 3: A tragic death

This is a personal experience of mine. When I was about 19 or 20, I decided to call on a girl I'd known at school. I'll call her Julie (not her real name). She lived a few miles away, and it had been quite a while since I'd last seen her – perhaps two or three years. When I arrived at her home, I was given unexpected and very bad news: she'd died, unexpectedly, the night before, or perhaps in the early hours of that very day – I'm not sure. I don't know the precise circumstances of her death, but she had a history of occasional epileptic seizures. If I remember rightly, I was told that she'd had a fit and somehow suffocated.

Naturally, one might wonder whether there was something 'psychic' or paranormal about the fact that my visit occurred so close to the time of Julie's unexpected death. However, there seemed to be nothing unusual about my decision to call on her. I didn't, for example, have a sudden, inexplicable feeling that I *must* see her. Secondly, for me, it was a one-off event. I don't regularly turn up at the homes of former acquaintances, only to be told that they've unexpectedly died. Therefore, this may have simply been a matter of coincidence.

## Case 4: A cyclist's experience

This report came to me from a Dundee-based man called Malcolm Hastie (real name). He had a friend called Watson Webster, who was a member of his cycling club in the late 1950s. In 1959, Webster moved to Corby, and Hastie hadn't heard of him since that time. But on a summer's evening, three years before writing to me, Hastie was almost home from a cycle run when the name 'Watson Webster' came into his mind for no reason. To his astonishment, he turned a corner and saw his old acquaintance standing in the middle of the street. It transpired that, unbeknown to Hastie, Webster's father-in-law lived in the same street as Hastie and had recently died. Webster had come up for the funeral.

Was it merely a coincidence that Hastie thought of Watson Webster and then saw him very shortly after? Maybe. Another possibility is that some form of extrasensory perception (ESP) was involved.

## Case 5: A French connection

This is another report from Malcolm Hastie. Some years ago, he was invited to visit Dundee's twin city in France, Orleans. While there, he would be required to make a speech, in French, before a large crowd. His French wasn't bad, but for this task, he thought he would contact his old French teacher, although they hadn't been in touch since Hastie left school in 1956. He was going to ask whether what he'd written down was correct.

Hastie was about to pick up the phone when it rang. A voice at the other end said, 'You may not remember me, but this is your old French master, D. B. Smith, speaking.' Smith explained that he was writing his memoirs about his childhood days and was looking for a collective noun to describe the huge mass of cyclists who would pour out of a local mill each evening. He remembered that, over the years, Hastie had featured regularly in the cycling column of the *Dundee Courier*, which he read. So Smith decided to take a chance and ring his former pupil.

## Case 6: Lucky 7s

In her 2001 book *Time Storms*, Jenny Randles relates an experience from 1999 involving her and her mother (pp. 137-8). The latter did the Lottery each week, using the same numbers each time. But in four years, she'd won nothing. The mother and daughter were in a shop paying a bill. It came to £7.77, and the assistant commented that this must be 'your lucky number'. When they returned to the car, they discovered that a vehicle parked beside it had a number plate including '777'. Furthermore, as they were about to drive away, Randles noticed that the mileage indicator in their car was displaying a number ending in 777. Her mother tried playing 7 in all the Lottery options that weekend, and she won a modest sum.

## Case 7: Synchronicity in the life of Raymond E. Fowler

Raymond Fowler was born in Massachusetts in 1933. He's a UFO researcher and author of various books, including *SynchroFile*, which details a multitude of synchronistic experiences that he's had in his life, and which he thinks statisticians would be hard-pressed to explain. The following are some examples.

In 1955, Fowler married a British woman, Margaret, whom he met while serving in England, in the United States Air Force. After he left the USAF, he and Margaret eventually settled in Wenham, Massachusetts. In 1996, Margaret's 96-year-old mother, by then a widow, was admitted to a nursing home in England, and her house was put up for sale. It was bought by a couple called Howard and Margery (or *Marjorie* – Fowler's spelling is inconsistent regarding this). In February 1997, Margaret made a sentimental visit to the house, receiving a warm welcome from the new owners. Margaret learned from Margery that her cousin's husband's sister, Evelyn (now deceased), had lived in a house in Wenham, Massachusetts. Amazingly, it was directly across the road from Raymond and Margaret Fowler's home. Furthermore, it transpired that Evelyn's brother-in-law (now deceased) was named *Raymond Fowle*. As if that weren't enough, Margaret learned that Margery's cousin Irene lived in the town of Essex, Massachusetts, just four houses away from where the Fowlers' son David was then living (Fowler, 2004, pp. 1-4).

While jogging in a state park in September 1999 and changing stations on his headset radio, Fowler turned to one where the host said that he would like to go 'jogging in the park' (*ibid.*, p. 12).

On 12 January 2000, Fowler was thinking of arranging an appointment with his dentist for a routine teeth-cleaning session. Looking at his records, he discovered that his last appointment had been on *June 28*, 1999. At that point, he noticed that the clock was reading *6:28* (*ibid.*, p. 21).

On the evening of 7 January 2001, Fowler and his wife were watching the film *The Sound of Music*, which includes a thunderstorm scene. At the same time, a real thunderstorm was occurring, although Fowler states that they're exceedingly rare in January (*ibid.*, p. 22).

Of course, taken individually, these incidents in Fowler's life could be put down to chance. And the fact that he's able to cite multiple instances could be attributed to the confirmation bias: his being on the lookout for such correspondences. However, I'm not sure that this satisfactorily explains the very large number of incidents that he's recorded in his book.

## Case 8: An old-fashioned helicopter

Christopher O'Brien is an American author and researcher with a particular interest in the cattle mutilation phenomenon. He had a synchronistic experience when he was living in the San Luis Valley, which runs from south-central Colorado into northern New Mexico. He has mentioned it in at least three of his books: *Secrets of the Mysterious Valley* (2007, pp. 100-3); *Stalking the Tricksters* (2009, pp. 69-73); *Stalking the Herd* (2014, pp. 292-4).

In 1993, O'Brien spoke to members of a family called Sutherland about a bull of theirs that had been found dead and mutilated in June 1980. The previous evening, they'd heard a helicopter flying slowly south over their property. Then, 15-20 minutes later, they heard it again and saw it rising from the pasture where the dead bull would be found the following morning. It was mustard-yellow in colour, old-fashioned in appearance, and seemed to be lacking any markings. It flew back over their house, towards the north. They made extensive enquiries, but were unable to discover where it had come from. They were told that a helicopter of that type would be extremely rare and would be highly expensive to keep airworthy.

The day after he visited the Sutherlands – i.e. some 13 years after the aforementioned incidents – O'Brien was at home, reviewing and typing up his interview notes, when he heard, and then saw, a helicopter that matched what the Sutherlands had seen in 1980. There were also other witnesses to the sighting. He notes that ever since that experience, he's been totally convinced that a tricksterish and paranormal energy, force, or entity is manipulating coincidence and creating synchronicity.

## Case 9: Experiences with owls

In his 2015 book *The Messengers*, Mike Clelland mentions a couple of intriguing experiences that he had in the company of a young woman called Kristen (pp. 12-4). In the autumn of 2006, they spent a night out camping in the mountains near Clelland's then home, although they hardly knew each other at that point. They spoke of their spiritual beliefs and insights, and there came a point in the conversation when Clelland felt a strong and 'hugely life affirming' connection with Kristen. Just then, an owl swooped over them. It was only a few feet above their heads. A second owl appeared, and then a third. For more than an hour, the three owls circled and swooped silently over the couple.

Clelland and Kristen went out again for a night's camping a few days later, this time in a different part of the mountains. Clelland suggested, as a way of warming themselves up before settling down for the night, that they should ascend a gentle, rounded hill. They reached the top, and, within seconds, three owls appeared and flew around them. After perching on some nearby branches, the owls eventually landed on the ground, within a few yards of the couple, and stared at them, the whole thing lasting around 30 minutes.

Nearly three years later, Clelland referred back to the initial experience and asked Kristen whether she remembered what they'd been talking about when the first owl appeared. She explained that she'd been trying to articulate her deepest beliefs about God.

## Case 10: The curse of 'Flight 191'

In the West, superstition has it that 13 is an unlucky number, and it may be avoided in some situations. For instance, there may be no 'Room 13' in some hotels, or a high building may have no floor numbered 13. In other parts of the world, different numbers are associated with good or bad luck. For example, in Japan, *nine* is reputed to be a bad luck number. When spoken aloud in Japanese, it sounds like 'suffering'.[3]

The numbering of aircraft flights is usually based on the direction of travel, with north and eastbound flights being given even numbers, and south and westbound flights being given odd numbers. As indicated below, a particular flight number – 191 – has been associated with several crashes, inviting speculation that it's an 'unlucky' or 'cursed' flight number. And, of course, 191 is an anagram of 911 ('nine eleven'). The stigma associated with 'Flight 191' has reportedly induced some airlines to avoid using the number.

*Aeroflot Flight 191, 5 March 1963*

Aeroflot Flight 191 was a Soviet domestic passenger flight from Vnukovo International Airport (near Moscow) to Ashgabat International Airport in Turkmenistan, with a stop-over at Krasnovodsk, now known as Turkmenbashi, which is also in Turkmenistan. On 5 March 1963, the Ilyushin Il-18V aircraft encountered a dust storm on its approach to Ashgabat International Airport. The flight should have been diverted elsewhere because of the storm. But that wasn't suggested by air traffic controllers, and the pilots didn't seek updated weather information. In the event, the plane collided with power lines and approach lights, crashing some 250 metres short of the runway. A fire erupted. Of the 54 people on board, 12 died (all eight members of the cockpit crew and four passengers).[4]

*X-15 Flight 3-65-97, 15 November 1967*

This was a research flight of a North American Aviation X-15 rocket-powered aircraft. At an altitude of 230,000 feet, it entered a Mach 5 spin. It disintegrated at 62,000 feet near Cuddeback Lake, California. Its pilot, USAF Major Michael J. Adams, was killed. Since this was the 191st flight of the X-15 programme, it has sometimes been referred to as Flight 191.[5]

*Prinair Flight 191, 24 June 1972*

On the night of 24 June 1972, a Prinair DeHavilland Heron, operating as Flight 191, flew from Luis Muñoz Marín International Airport in San Juan on the north coast of Puerto Rico to Mercedita Airport in Ponce, close to the south coast. On their approach, the pilots thought they saw an airport vehicle on the runway. They aborted the landing, but unfortunately that caused the aircraft to stall and crash. Five of the 20 people on board were killed, including the pilot and co-pilot. Although the USA's National Transportation

Safety Board (NTSB) initially deemed that a vehicle on the runway had been responsible,[6] it was later revealed that the driver of the supposed vehicle had left the airport before the crash.

*American Airlines Flight 191, 25 May 1979*

On the afternoon of 25 May 1979, a McDonnell Douglas DC-10 took off from Chicago's O'Hare International Airport. Its intended destination was Los Angeles International Airport in California. However, its left engine detached, and the plane crashed less than a mile from the end of the runway. All 271 people on board were killed, plus two on the ground, making it the USA's deadliest aviation accident. The NTSB deemed that the crash had resulted from inadequate maintenance of the aircraft.[7]

*Delta Airlines Flight 191, 2 August 1985*

A Lockheed L-1011 took off from Fort Lauderdale-Hollywood International Airport in Florida. Its ultimate destination was Los Angeles, but its route involved a stop-over in Dallas, Texas. Over Louisiana, thunderstorms began to form in the path of the aircraft, but things proceeded normally *en route* to Dallas. However, as the plane lined up for landing, it entered a storm and experienced conditions that resulted in its hitting the ground in a field short of the runway. It bounced back up into the air, crossed a highway, with one of its engines hitting a car and killing the occupant. The plane bounced into the air once more, and then veered into water tanks on the perimeter of the airport, whereupon the tail section spun off. The forward section of the plane, from the nose to seating row 34, was destroyed in the collision with the water tanks. Some 137 people died. (I've approximated here, since sources differ slightly on the precise figure.)[8,9]

*Comair Flight 5191, 27 August 2006*

On 27 August 2006, a CRJ-100 aircraft bound for Atlanta, Georgia, failed to become properly airborne during an attempted take-off from Blue Grass Airport in Lexington, Kentucky. It ran off the end of the runway, lifted momentarily, and then smashed into an embankment, a fence, and some trees. Having broken apart, it came to a stop in a field and was engulfed in flames. Fifty people were on board. All of them perished, except the first officer, James Polehinke, who was badly injured.[10]

There were two runways at the airport, numbered 22 and 26. The plane should have taken off from the former, but a mistake was made, and the aircraft taxied onto runway 26, which was too short for the plane. Various factors may have contributed to this catastrophic error. For example, in violation of Federal Aviation Administration (FAA) rules, there'd been unnecessary talk between the captain and the first officer, which may have made them less attentive to their checks and procedures; and there was criticism of the airport regarding inadequate signage and runway markings.

Readers may have noticed that the flight number was 5191 rather than 191. However, in air traffic control communications, it was called 'Comair 191'.

*JetBlue Flight 191, 27 March 2012*

This was a commercial passenger flight from New York to Las Vegas. On the day in question, the Airbus A320 plane was diverted to an airport in Amarillo, Texas, after the captain suffered an apparent mental breakdown and was restrained by passengers. There were no deaths.[11]

## COMMENTS

If we reject the sceptical view that all seemingly synchronistic events are purely chance occurrences, what are we to make of cases of the type cited above? Arguably, Jung's contention that synchronicity is real but 'acausal' (i.e. that it doesn't involve 'cause and effect') is rather vague or mystical. Another possibility is that some sort of higher intelligence is capable of orchestrating events and bringing about synchronicity, which is evidently Christopher O'Brien's view (see Case 8, above). In a similar vein, Jenny Randles (2001, p. 148) suggests that synchronicities may reflect an undercurrent in which consciousness shapes reality into patterns. This is a matter that I'll return to in the final chapter of this book.

Regarding Case 10, I'm doubtful whether it's anything more than a matter of chance that several ill-fated aircraft have been labelled Flight 191. Although the cumulative loss of life has been tragically high, the number of incidents is quite small. Furthermore, over the years, many flights numbered 191 no doubt passed off without incident.

# CHAPTER 3

# THE PARANORMAL

The notion of a curse implies some sort of malign influence on a *target* (e.g. a person or a family). Imagine, for instance, that someone curses Joe and that, three days later, he crashes his car and is killed. This raises several possibilities: (1) The two events may be unrelated (i.e. Joe's fatal accident may have had nothing to do with the curse). (2) There *is* a connection between the curse and Joe's death, but there's nothing paranormal about it. Perhaps Joe knew about the curse, which made him very anxious, inducing him to drink heavily, and he was drunk at the time of the crash. (3) At the time of the accident, Joe succumbed to a telepathic influence that adversely affected his driving. (4) The curse unleashed a mysterious *physical* force. For example, Joe's steering wheel may have been suddenly wrenched from his control and jerked in the wrong direction, causing him to collide with an oncoming lorry.

Of course, possibilities (3) and (4) entail something paranormal. One might ask whether there's any independent evidence for such phenomena. The answer is 'yes'; and in this chapter, I'll cite examples. First, though, I'll define some terms.

## TERMINOLOGY

*Psychical research* is the scientific investigation of phenomena that are supposedly paranormal. The manifestations themselves, if deemed genuine, are often referred to as *psi phenomena* or simply *psi*. There are several strands to psychical research, such as laboratory-based experimental work, the study of mediumship, and the investigation of spontaneous cases (precognitive dreams, apparitions, poltergeist phenomena, etc.). The term *parapsychology* is sometimes employed as a synonym of psychical research. But in the UK, at least, it tends to be used in a narrower sense, to refer to experimental psi research carried out in laboratory-type settings. In terms of this distinction, all parapsychologists could be described as psychical researchers, but not all psychical researchers would be classed as parapsychologists. For example, investigators who focus on spontaneous cases, such as poltergeist disturbances, could be described as psychical researchers. But if they don't carry out laboratory-type research, they might not be regarded as parapsychologists.

*Extrasensory perception* (ESP) is the acquisition of information by paranormal means rather than through the usual senses. Judging from reports, it often occurs automatically and unconsciously – that is, without any conscious intention on the part of those involved. Various types of ESP can be distinguished.

*Telepathy* is direct mind-to-mind communication. For example, someone might sense the feelings or pick up information from a distant loved one, or might transmit a mental image to that person. At times, telepathy may involve more than just two people. Telepathy may occur among non-human animals, and evidence suggests that it can occur between people and their pet animals (Sheldrake, 1999).

The word *clairvoyance* comes from French and literally means 'clear seeing'. Psychical researchers use it to refer to a form of ESP in which someone acquires information about a physical situation elsewhere in a seemingly direct way that doesn't entail telepathy. Imagine, for instance, that I get a mental image of a supposedly extinct volcano erupting in a very remote and uninhabited part of the world, and that it transpires that such an eruption occurred at the very the time that I visualized it. That's the sort of situation that might be described as clairvoyance.

*Precognition* refers to acquiring information, paranormally, about the future. For example, imagine an experiment in which a subject, Mary, is asked to guess, in advance, the identity of a letter of the alphabet that will be randomly selected by a computer. This process is repeated until, say, 100 such guesses have been recorded. If Mary is capable of precognition, she may score significantly above (or below) what would be expected by chance. However, another possibility would be that *psychokinesis* (a 'mind over matter' effect) came into play, enabling Mary, presumably unconsciously, to influence the selection of target letters or to make the computer record an incorrect number of supposedly correct guesses.

There are reports of people temporarily experiencing their surroundings as if they'd gone back in time. Incidents of this type are popularly known as 'time-slips'. Psychical researchers might refer to the phenomenon as *retrocognition*. The late Andrew MacKenzie (1997, pp. 3-30) discussed an incident from 1957 in which three youths possibly perceived a Suffolk village (Kersey) as it had been centuries earlier. The main informant was a man called William Laing, who first contacted MacKenzie about the incident in 1988. Michael Crowley, one of the others, couldn't remember the occasion clearly, but provided some corroboration of Laing's recollections. Ray Baker, the third person, seemed to recall little or nothing of the village.

## EXPERIMENTAL EVIDENCE FOR PSI

### Extrasensory perception (ESP)

Reports on experimental ESP and psychokinesis research tend to be couched in rather technical language, but Dean Radin, a parapsychologist based in the USA, provides a readable account of it in his 1997 and 2006 books *The Conscious Universe* and *Entangled Minds*. Regarding ESP, he refers, for example, to what are known as ganzfeld experiments. ('Ganzfeld', a German word, means 'whole field'.)

The procedure is broadly as follows, although there can be variations: A person designated as the 'receiver' – let's call him Bob – is seated comfortably. Continuous white noise is played into his ears via headphones, and red light is shone on his face through translucent hemispheres placed over his eyes, the aim being to foster a psi-conducive state of mind. A 10-minute relaxation recording might be played to facilitate this. After a while, the 'sending' process begins, which is an attempt to convey impressions of a target item to Bob. A target pack containing four possible target items (pictures, say) will have been randomly selected from a large pool of such packs, and one of the four items will have been randomly selected as the actual target. Another person (the 'sender'), located elsewhere, views the target item. The sending phase lasts 15 minutes or more, after which Bob removes the eyeshades and turns off the red lamp. The white noise is also turned off. Bob is then shown copies of the four potential target items, one of which was the actual target. This is done by someone who doesn't know what the target was. Alternatively, if an automated system is employed, a computer displays the four potential targets to Bob in a random order via a video monitor. He's asked to rank them from 1 to 4 according to the degree to which they match the impressions he had during the sending phase. A direct hit is recorded if he ranks the actual target item as No. 1. A hit rate of 25 per cent is expected by chance. So, if he participates in 32 sessions, he would be expected to obtain about eight direct hits. A significantly higher (or lower) score could indicate the operation of psi.

The terms 'sender' and 'receiver' imply that the experiment is a test of telepathy, something entailing the transmission of information from one person to another. However, if the receiver's hit rate is significantly different from what would be expected by chance, it could be that he or she has obtained information via clairvoyance or precognition, and that no sender was necessary.

In his 2006 book, Radin states that the overall findings from ganzfeld research strongly support the existence of ESP. He refers to a study by Bem, Palmer, and Broughton (2001), who looked at a batch of recent ganzfeld studies and found that experiments adhering to the standard format, with visual targets, collectively yielded odds of 5,000 to 1 against the outcome being due to chance.

## Psychokinesis (PK)

Clear-cut object movements have been witnessed in poltergeist and haunting cases, and examples will be cited later in this chapter. In laboratory-based psychokinesis (PK) experiments, on the other hand, the emphasis has often been on what's called *micro-PK*: psychokinetic effects that aren't directly observable, but which can be inferred statistically. For example, Radin's 2006 book discusses experiments in which subjects have tried to affect the output of electronic devices known as random number generators (RNGs). Taking the various RNG studies into account, he contends that the effect has been small in magnitude but highly significant statistically.

Ideas from quantum physics have been incorporated in some parapsychological theories (see Radin, 2006, pp. 250-74). For example, 'observational theory' assumes that the act of observing a quantum event can affect its outcome. Radin refers to experiments in which previously recorded, but unobserved, random bits (1s and 0s) were later observed, but with subjects being instructed to aim, for example, for an excess of 1s. He states that the results were successful, and he refers to the act of observation as 'retroactively' influencing quantum events. However, I'm not sure whether it's necessary to infer a process that works backwards in time. Perhaps the unobserved random bits remain in some sort of indeterminate state right up to the point when they're observed. Or maybe the sequence of bits is psychokinetically changed at the very point of being observed! These notions are, of course, far removed from our conventional way of thinking about the world.

Since the 1950s, there've been numerous studies bearing on the question of whether attempts at distant influence and 'distant healing' can have a real effect.[1] An experiment of this type might, for instance, involve a subject connected to equipment that monitors his or her physiology, and where, in another room, there's a person whose task it is to try to influence the subject's level of arousal during randomly chosen periods, not known to the subject (at least, not by normal means). Positive results have been reported, and they're consistent with the notion that some people, at least, can exert a psychokinetic effect on others. However, as Mario Varvoglis has pointed out, in respect of distant healing, there's a catch:

> ... what if patients are not truly isolated from the healer's mind? True, the subjects in these experiments have no 'normal' way of distinguishing influence from non-influence periods – but what if they have a 'paranormal' means for knowing this? While they cannot hear, see or sense the healer, nor logically infer which periods are 'influence' vs. 'noninfluence', perhaps they really do have this knowledge – on the basis of a telepathic contact with the healer. At the moment the influence period begins, healers undoubtedly have thoughts like 'okay, now I must focus on the person'; when the rest period begins, she or he may think 'now I can relax'. If there is some telepathic rapport between the two persons, then one (the patient) may simply be acting as a 'receiver' in a telepathy experiment, unconsciously picking up information from the 'sender' and then inducing slight shifts in his or her own physiology. In this case, we are back to a form of self-induced healing – a telepathically induced placebo effect!

> Am [I] splitting hairs here? What's the difference between telepathically triggered self-healing, vs. a healing truly based on another person's influence, i.e., based on psychokinesis (mind-over-matter)? Well, there are several theoretical issues here; but there's also

at least one important practical concern. In real instances of illness or disease, a patient may not have the resources, mentally, psychologically or physically, to induce self-healings, even given the kinds of suggestions which usually trigger placebo effects. By contrast, if healing – and not just healing suggestions – really comes from an external source, then a vital, confident healer could still input positive 'energy' into the patient's organism and restore health.

So, it would be nice to know if lab results are pointing to telepathy or to psychokinesis. Given the complexity of human minds, and the different possible interactions between them, it would be very difficult to answer this question as long as the 'patient' – the recipient of the healing effect – is a person. But researchers have also been exploring psychokinesis (PK) on other kinds of biological systems, which are not likely to 'self-heal' through suggestion, placebos etc. If we find that healers can induce such 'bio-PK' effects on these simpler organisms, then there's a good chance that the healing effects observed with humans indeed are based on a true 'healing force'.[2]

Regarding Varvoglis's last paragraph, there is some evidence of psychokinetic effects on non-human animals, although its quality has been questioned.[3] But I must say, in passing, that I don't approve of experiments that involve subjecting sentient creatures to stress, pain, and death.

A study published by Leonard Leibovici in 2001 looked at the clinical outcome for 3,393 patients who, between 1990 and 1996, had been diagnosed at an Israeli hospital as having a bloodstream infection.[4] In July 2000, they were randomly allocated to either a control group or an intervention group. A 'remote, retroactive intercessory prayer' was said for the well-being and full recovery of the latter group. Mortality was slightly lower in the intervention group, although the difference wasn't statistically significant. However, the length of stay in hospital and duration of fever were significantly shorter for the intervention group.

Taken at face value, Leibovici's study suggests something quite remarkable: that an intervention made *now*, such as praying for patients who were unwell years previously, can work *backwards* in time with a beneficial effect! But of course, the results may have been a statistical fluke, and one might wish to see the study replicated in some way before coming to firm conclusions.

Since the prayer is described as having been 'intercessory', I presume that it called on God's help. However, it's possible that the retroactive psychokinetic influence, if there was one, came from the person doing the praying. Another possibility is that the outcome resulted not from the prayer as such, but from hope, on Leibovici's part, that the results of his study would be positive. Again, one might attribute this to retroactive PK. But I don't think we're compelled to assume that any psychokinetic effect must have worked backwards in time. It's conceivable that, as a result of psi, the allocation of patients to the control group and intervention group *wasn't* truly random. In other words, more patients with a positive outcome may have been allocated to the intervention group. In effect, then, the results of the study could have been 'rigged' by paranormal means!

In 1972, some members of the Toronto Society for Psychical Research set about trying to elicit psychokinesis. They created an identity for a fictitious spirit communicator: a 17th-century English aristocratic, whom they named 'Philip'. This was to help get round 'ownership resistance', a hypothesized reluctance that people might have to identifying themselves as the source of paranormal activity. They met frequently over an extended period, and physical phenomena were eventually manifested, such as raps and large movements of a table. However, they didn't seriously believe that a disembodied spirit was responsible. The case is discussed in Iris Owen and Margaret Sparrow's 1976 book *Conjuring up Philip: An Adventure in Psychokinesis.*

## SPONTANEOUS PSI

In the experimental research mentioned above, the intended psychic influence was either neutral (e.g. seeing whether a person in Room A could affect the physiological arousal of a subject in Room B), or intended to be beneficial (an attempt to heal members of a target group). The fact that positive results have been reported suggests that a mental influence of a telepathic or psychokinetic kind really can occur. Therefore, regarding ill-wishes and curses, it's quite plausible that they will sometimes harm their targets – by, for example, inducing (or aggravating) illnesses, damaging property, or frightening the victims with ghostly phenomena. Before turning (in the next chapter) to specific cases that seem to reflect the operation of ill-will or cursing, I'll cite here some examples of spontaneous paranormal activity (i.e. paranormal activity that occurs without deliberate prompting). A large array of such manifestations has been reported over the years, and – to keep things reasonably succinct – I'll be very selective, and confine myself mainly to haunting and poltergeist cases.

## Occasional psychokinesis

Mary Rose Barrington (1926-2020) was an intelligent, respected and longstanding member of the UK's Society for Psychical Research. 'Jott' is an acronym that she derived from the expression 'just one of those things'. In her book *JOTT* (p. 4), she uses it to refer to cases of 'spatial discontinuity' (e.g. where an item is found to be unaccountably missing from its usual location and is later found in an unexpected place).

Barrington divided jott phenomena into two main classes: 'jottles' and 'oddjotts'. She defined a jottle as an 'unwitnessed displacement', although she noted that, in rare cases, 'the article is seen to disappear from sight or is felt to elude the grasp, but its displacement to another location is not witnessed' (*ibid.*, p. 4). It's worth noting that, in Barrington's view, articles that jottle don't move – instead, they 'de-actualize' and 're-actualize' (*ibid.*, pp. 166-7).

Jottles seem to be far more common than oddjotts (discussed below). The manifestations take various forms (*ibid.*, p. 5): (1) A 'walkabout' entails an article disappearing from its expected location and turning up elsewhere. Of course, someone might misplace an item in a moment of absent-mindedness or distraction, with nothing paranormal being involved. But in respect of walkabouts and other types of jottle, Barrington cites intriguing cases that seem to defy a normal explanation. (2) In a 'turn-up', an article from an uncertain location appears where it wasn't before. (3) In a 'comeback', an item disappears from where it was known to have been, and it's later found back in that same place. (4) In a 'flyaway', an item disappears from where it was known to have been, never to be seen again. (5) A 'windfall' entails an item, of unknown origin, appearing in a place where it couldn't have been before it was found there. (6) A 'trade-in' is where an article disappears from where it was known to have been and is replaced (perhaps sometime later) by a similar item, of unknown origin, appearing in more or less in the same location.

These categories aren't all mutually exclusive. For example, one person's flyaway could be someone else's windfall.

Barrington stated that the main feature of an *oddjott* 'is matter manifesting in ways inconsistent with the laws and expectations generally believed to govern the material world' (*ibid.*, pp. 88-9). She cited an experience of her own (*ibid.*, pp. 89-90): After being washed and then retrieved from her tumble drier, a duvet cover was found to be zipped up and inside out. She noted: 'If [it] had gone into the wash fully zipped up it could not have turned itself inside out. If it had gone in unzipped, […] then how could a washer or a drier have forced the closure of [a] particularly difficult little zip?'

Jott-type incidents often occur in poltergeist and haunt cases, which – by definition – involve recurrent phenomena. For example, a case that I investigated in Scotland included what (in terms of Barrington's classification of jottles) could be described as a 'trade-in': One morning, a man discovered that three folded £20 notes had disappeared from a metal container in his living room. He returned to his house at lunchtime that day, and there were three £20 notes laid out on the coffee table. They appeared new and weren't creased.

In many cases, a jott might be a one-off incident. But some of Barrington's informants had had more than one experience, and could, perhaps, be described as jott-prone. One might surmise that, unconsciously, they tended to manifest or catalyse psychokinetic effects. A highly jott-prone person could be described as a 'poltergeist focus'. In other words, in terms of the underlying agency and mechanisms, there may be no fundamental difference between jott cases and full-blown poltergeist incidents.

**Recurrent manifestations**

If a person or place has been cursed, and if this results in paranormal phenomena being experienced, it's perhaps likely that the manifestations will be recurrent and perhaps take the form of 'haunting' or poltergeist-type phenomena.

Psychical researchers use the expression 'haunting' or 'haunt' to refer to recurrent paranormal phenomena associated with particular places rather than specific people. The manifestations may be wholly sensory (e.g. sensing a presence, hearing footsteps, or seeing an apparition), or they may include incidents of a more physical character, such as the displacement of objects, opening or closing of doors, and disturbance of bedclothes. Judging from reports, some cases continue for many years, although the phenomena might be intermittent. Various theories have been proposed to explain hauntings. A traditional notion, probably more popular with amateur 'ghost hunters' than with scientific psychical researchers, is that the phenomena are produced by the 'earthbound spirits' of people who once lived in, or were associated with, the haunted location. Another view is that past events can leave an impression on a place, which can be 'replayed' in certain circumstances. Others have suggested, for example, that localized magnetic fields can affect the nervous system of people in 'haunted' places, generating strange sensations and hallucinations.

The word 'poltergeist' comes from German words meaning 'noisy spirit', although 'Spukphenome' is apparently the preferred term in Germany itself. Poltergeist cases entail recurrent physical phenomena, such as the movement of objects, rapping and knocking sounds, and the breakage of glass and crockery. The phenomena are often associated with the presence of a particular living person (the 'poltergeist focus'), typically someone who is relatively young (e.g. a pubescent girl or teenager). Indeed, some researchers describe poltergeist phenomena as 'recurrent spontaneous psychokinesis' (RSPK), the assumption being that the phenomena are generated (most likely, unconsciously) by the focal person. Although poltergeist disturbances are typically brief, perhaps lasting no more than a few weeks or months, some long-running cases have been noted. For example, Ciaran O'Keefe (2021) describes a case from Battersea, in London, that ran from 1956 to 1968.

It's not always easy to draw a hard and fast line between hauntings and poltergeist episodes. For example, apparitions are sometimes seen in poltergeist cases, and, as noted, physical phenomena (usually relatively minor) are often reported in cases of haunting. Haunt manifestations are generally more subtle and less 'in your face' than poltergeist phenomena. For example, if witnesses in Room A hear sounds suggestive of objects being moved about in Room B, they may find nothing out of place if they go into Room B to check (see Case 1, below). In a poltergeist case, however, they may indeed find considerable disturbance of objects in Room B.

In poltergeist cases, the manifestations may follow the focal person or afflicted family from one residence to another. This seems less common in clear-cut haunting cases, although it may have occurred in the case of Margaret Black (see Case 2, below).

In writings on poltergeist cases, one sometimes see mention of '*the* poltergeist' or '*a* poltergeist', but I think these expressions should be avoided, since they could be taken to mean that some sort of discrete entity or spirit is behind the phenomena, which may or may not be the case. Therefore, I prefer more neutral expressions, such as 'poltergeist phenomena' or 'poltergeist activity'.

Readers may already be familiar with certain well-publicized cases, such as one at Enfield on the northern fringe of London in 1977-9. Therefore, to avoid a weary, 'Oh no, not that again!' reaction, here are outlines of some less well-known haunt and poltergeist cases, including three from my own files.

*Case 1: Haunting*

This case was brought to my attention in the summer of 1999. Pseudonyms have been substituted for the names of those involved. My informants, Lorna and Isobel, experienced a variety of unusual phenomena while working as cleaners at industrial premises in eastern Scotland. Unsettled by their experiences, they'd recently given up their jobs there.

Isobel and another cleaner, Sean, started working at the premises around October 1995. Their jobs required them to go into the workplace fairly early in the morning, before the main workforce arrived. After a few uneventful weeks, Sean reported phenomena, such as hearing whispering on some stairs. And after she'd been there about a year, Isobel heard a woman's voice saying, 'Shh! Shh!', as if someone were being told to keep quiet. She subsequently had other unusual experiences. For instance, at one point, she and Sean were present when a door closed unexpectedly. On another occasion, they heard something being dragged across the floor of the main office above. But when Isobel went upstairs and looked into the room, she saw nothing out of place.

From January 1999, shortly after she joined Isobel at the workplace, until June of that year, when she left, Lorna experienced various phenomena, such as hearing footsteps, sensing a presence, and having a door shut in her face. In June, she took a mini-cassette tape recorder into the workplace on three occasions, and it recorded sounds (of apparent talking, laughing, etc.) that she and Isobel hadn't heard at the time. (This type of manifestation is known as the *electronic voice phenomenon* or $EVP$.)

In a written account that Isobel prepared for me, she mentioned several other people who'd reportedly experienced odd events at the premises. I wrote to three of them, as well as to Sean, asking whether they would provide statements about their experiences. But I received no replies.

If the phenomena were paranormal, could they have been created, in part, by Isobel and Lorna themselves? Both women described previous experiences that may have been paranormal, and Lorna, at least, who had a sizeable collection of books on the subject, had been interested in the paranormal for several years.

## Case 2: Haunting

Margaret Black (pseudonym) was in her forties when I was in contact with her, some 20 years ago. She was a graduate with a professional job. She was in good health. Before the events described below, she hadn't experienced anything that seemed paranormal. But she went on to experience manifestations at two successive homes, the first of which I'll describe as the 'old house'. The next house was where she was living when I was in touch with her. I'll refer to it as the 'new house'.

For clarity, I'll divide Margaret's occupancy of the old house into two periods: the 'early period' (approximately two and a half years, from August 1991 until early 1994); and the 'later period' (from March 1994, when she got married, to early 1998, when she and her family moved to the new house).

During the early period at the old house, she was the only one living there, although she acquired two kittens towards the end of 1991. The house belonged to Margaret's employers. It was built of stone, and stood alone, close to fields, across the road from an active Royal Air Force base in the UK. There were trees nearby, but not close enough for branches to bang against the building in windy weather. During this early phase, Margaret experienced various phenomena. For example, one night, in the downstairs bedroom, she heard light, regular taps, which seemed to be coming from the ceiling. Every time she switched the light on, they stopped; but they resumed when she switched the light off. After a few minutes, she left the room and went to sleep upstairs, as she was beginning to feel uneasy.

Starting very soon after she moved into the house, and recurring throughout the whole of her occupancy, there were times when Margaret would be working at the kitchen sink and would have a strong feeling that someone was standing behind her, very close, looking over her left shoulder. Starting during the early period and continuing during the later period, there were telephone problems; and during the later period, there were other malfunctions with electrical equipment, such as a radio coming on by itself.

During the later period, there were further auditory phenomena, and also visual manifestations. For example, one evening, while Margaret was sitting on a sofa, watching television in the lounge, she noticed something out of the corner of her eye. But because she wore glasses, she didn't bother to turn round, presuming that light from the television set was reflecting off her spectacles. Suddenly, her son, then about two years old, who'd been playing on the floor, pointed at the sofa and shouted, 'Look, mummy, look!' She did so; and, with her son following it with his finger, she saw something very nebulous, like cigarette smoke, roll off the sofa, move along the floor and disappear under a table by the window. She and her son looked under the table, but there was nothing to be seen. However, she had a fleeting mental picture of a little boy hiding there. The next time her son reported seeing something, she asked him what it was, and he replied that it was 'a little boy'. She asked for his name, and her son immediately said 'Thomas'.

Margaret spoke to a retired man who'd previously lived in the house for a long time, but he seemed rather incredulous when she mentioned 'Thomas'. But another former occupant told her something of interest: that she'd once seen what could be best described as nebulous forms dancing on the floor. This witness would have been a child at the time.

When I was in touch with Margaret, the old house was occupied by a married couple who'd recently had a son, the husband being a colleague of Margaret's. Not wishing to alarm them, Margaret hadn't told them about the unusual things experienced during her occupancy, and they hadn't spoken to her about anything odd happening there.

Although Margaret was beginning to feel uneasy about the phenomena, the main reason for her family moving to the new house in 1998 was to get away from aircraft noise. The new house had been built in 1994 and was on a small housing estate, several miles from the old house. Margaret's two sons reported some odd experiences. For example, one morning, she caught them crouching on the stairs, peering into their bedroom. Asked what they were doing, they said they'd heard one of the toys talk. Margaret herself also had some odd experiences at the house. For example, on occasions, she would smell cigarette smoke, although neither she nor her husband smoked; and at one point, she was coming out of the kitchen and passing the lounge door when she heard a very deep male voice saying what sounded like 'Hello!'

Margaret's husband provided a degree of corroboration regarding her experiences at the old house. For example, he'd personally witnessed some incidents in which electrical equipment malfunctioned. Regarding the new house, he appeared to have experienced no phenomena.

If electrical power requirements at the RAF station near the old house varied significantly over time, and if the base drew at least some of its supply from the source used by local residents, could that have produced fluctuations in the supply at the house, with transient effects on some of the electrical equipment there? Another possible source of influence may have been some sort of field or radiation-generating installation at the base. I raised these points in a letter to the station commander, but I received no reply. Margaret reported that a former RAF flight controller had 'told us that the radar station [at the base] was too far from the house to affect us.' But could radar transmissions from flying aircraft have had an effect?

*Case 3: Haunting*

In 2002, Jim Hunter (real name), then 62 and a retired civil engineer, informed me about a couple of apparitional experiences – no doubt linked – that occurred in the 1990s. His job was related to the oil industry. He worked on the construction of rigs and platforms in the UK, the Middle East, India, Indonesia and Azerbaijan. Before the incidents described below, he was, as he put it, a 'down-to-earth typical construction engineer, with rather dismissive opinions on paranormal events'.

He was staying in a hotel in the town of Ras-Al-Khaimah, some 150 kilometres north of Dubai, in the United Arab Emirates. He'd been at the hotel for about nine months and stayed in a small suite comprising a sitting room and bedroom. One night in mid-1994, he awoke, feeling the presence of someone in the bedroom. The atmosphere was cold. He switched on the bedside light and saw the figure of an Indian man standing at the end of the bed, looking in his direction. The figure appeared to be quite solid. It turned its back on him and walked through the wall that formed the gable end of the building. Not surprisingly, Jim felt pretty spooked, and he subsequently kept the light on for the rest of the night. He told a few people about it that morning when he went to work, and he received a lot of ribbing. He concluded that it had been a bad dream, although he asked the head waiter whether anyone had died in any of the rooms, and, in particular, in his suite (No. 304). The head waiter had been at the hotel for 25 years, but he said that he knew of no incident. The whole matter was slowly forgotten. Three months later, Jim was moved to another suite, as his rooms were going to be converted into a flat for the manager.

A year after Jim's ghostly experience, he and his colleagues had a visit from two graduate Indian engineers from the company's head office. One of them was allocated Room 303, a single room adjacent to Jim's former sitting room. (The bedroom in Jim's former suite was off the sitting room.) On his first morning at work, the Indian engineer and Jim's secretary came into Jim's office. The Indian man was in a state of severe agitation and looked awful. It turned out that he'd experienced what Jim had experienced a year before. He'd awoken to see an Indian man standing at the end of his bed. The figure then turned and walked through the wall into Jim's old suite. The engineer refused to be given another room and insisted on being moved to another hotel, which was arranged. Jim remained at the hotel for another year, without experiencing any further apparitional incidents, and he didn't hear of anyone else having such an experience.

*Case 4: Haunting*

In his book *Nights in Haunted Houses*, the late Peter Underwood described an interesting case concerning a council house on the Bilborough Estate in Nottingham (pp. 167-72). Shortly after Charles Hill and his two daughters and son moved in, Charles woke up one night to see the figure of a young man, dressed like a cricketer. A couple of nights later, he saw the apparition again. In addition, there were occasions when he heard the sound of a young man singing. Not long after his second sighting of the apparition, Charles' elder daughter, 17-year-old Sandra, saw the same figure, in daylight hours, on the stairs. The terrified family then abandoned the house.

Underwood and some fellow Ghost Club members conducted an overnight investigation at the house, accompanied by Charles and Sandra. (Underwood bequeathed his papers to the paranormal researcher and author Paul Adams, who informs me that the investigation took place in March 1968. It appears that 13 people participated and that Charles Hill and Sandra weren't the only non-GC members present.) Phenomena were experienced (e.g. the hearing of footsteps); and at one point, Underwood (but no one else) heard a sharp crack, similar to that of a pistol shot. Séances were conducted that night. During one of them, a man's name 'came through'. He claimed to be the ghost, and said that he loved Sandra! During another séance, Underwood asked, 'Did you commit suicide?' The reply was an emphatic 'Yes'.

Some months later, an elderly widow, then living in Bristol, was tracked down. Her surname matched one that had come up during the séances. She stated that she and her late son had formerly lived in the Nottingham house. He'd been happy, and often sang when he was in it. Tragically, though, he was involved in an accident that left him paralysed from the waist down. He eventually became depressed, and he committed suicide by shooting himself. He'd been interested in sport, particularly cricket, and he'd frequently dressed in cricket attire.

The Hills moved to another council house and weren't further bothered by ghostly phenomena. Another family moved into the vacated house. But they didn't report any disturbances. Underwood and his colleagues surmised that it had been Sandra's presence that had somehow triggered the phenomena.

In many cases of haunting, it's not clear who, or what, is behind the ghostly events, and any linking of the manifestations with the history of the place concerned might be largely conjectural. In this case, however, there are very clear parallels between the reported phenomena and the history of the house, as might be found in a fictional ghost story. As noted, at one point, Underwood heard a sound resembling that of a pistol shot. From an evidential point of view, it would be interesting to know whether he described it as such *before* learning that a former occupant of the house had shot himself there.

*Case 5: Poltergeist activity*

Between December 1966 and January 1967, poltergeist activity occurred at the Miami, Florida, warehouse of Tropication Arts, a wholesaler of Florida-themed novelty items (beer mugs, drinking glasses, alligator ashtrays, etc.).[5] The phenomena took the form of individual items, or boxes of items, falling from storage shelves for no apparent reason. In some instances, it seems that a fallen object had gone round, or over, one standing in its path. Many items were broken. There were multiple witnesses, including police officers and the psychical researcher William Roll (who made his first visit to the premises on 19 January). The disturbances peaked on Monday, 23 January, beginning as soon as the business opened for the day, with 52 separate incidents being logged.

It became evident that the 'focus' of the activity was a 19-year-old shipping clerk, Julio Vasquez, a Cuban refugee. However, he didn't seem to be the direct cause (in a normal sense), since he was sometimes under observation and nowhere near when things happened. Furthermore, no evidence of trickery (via, for example, the use of threads) was ever found. It was speculated that the phenomena were psychokinetic effects emanating from Vasquez, and related to repressed anger.

*Case 6: Poltergeist activity*

Andrew Nichols, an American psychical researcher, investigated a case in Jacksonville, Florida, on behalf of an insurance company (Nichols & Roll, 1998; Roll & Persinger, 2001). This was in connection with a claim related to water damage. The house in question was occupied by four people, spanning four generations of a family: (1) 62-year-old Mary Barton, (2) Mary's son, (3) Mary's 11-year-old granddaughter, and (4) Mary's mother, Lillian.

In early November 1996, there were rapping noises and then sprinklings of water on Lillian. Thereafter, all members of the household were wetted periodically, and occasionally soaked. Two plumbers were unable to find a leak, although both were wetted during their inspections, as was another contractor, who couldn't detect any problems with the air-conditioning ducts. At one point, three members of the household were drenched to such a degree that they took refuge in the family van on the driveway. A large amount of water then came from the house and splashed against the side of the vehicle.

There were also occasional object movements.

The disturbances occurred only when the 11-year-old girl was at home. But she was sometimes under observation at the time, or known to be in another part of the house. Therefore, it seemed that she wasn't producing the effects by trickery. 'EMFs' (electromagnetic fields, although I think the reference here is to *magnetic fields*) with a mean of 9.8 milligauss were detected in areas where phenomena had reportedly occurred, but the mean at control sites was within the normal range. Additionally, some transient readings of over 60 milligauss were recorded. High voltage transmission towers within a quarter of a mile of the house were a possible source of these field anomalies.

Hostility between the 11-year-old girl and Lillian (the child's great-grandmother) was evident to Nichols, and psychological tests suggested a high degree of aggressiveness in the relationships of the three female members of the household. Nichols suggested that the family seek counselling. In December 1996, Mary found a suicide note written by her granddaughter, and she arranged a psychiatric appointment for the girl. There was no further poltergeist activity after the child began psychotherapy in January 1997. It's unclear whether this was because of the treatment or because the manifestations had run their course.

*Case 7: Poltergeist activity*

In January 1975, the *Glasgow Herald* reported on a poltergeist case involving two council flats, one above the other, at Northgate Quadrant in the Balornock district of Glasgow.[6] The occupants of the lower flat were Mr and Mrs James Keenan and their son, with the Grieve family (mother, father, two sons, and Mrs Grieve's mother) living in the upper flat. Most of the information about the case relates to the Grieve family, and it seems that it was they who experienced most of the phenomena.

**Northgate Quadrant, Balornock**

Glasgow-based Archie Roy (1924-2012), who became a professor of astronomy in 1977, had a strong interest in psychical research. He became involved in the Balornock case in early 1975, and he witnessed phenomena at the Grieves' flat. He included a slightly muddled account of the case in his 1990 book *A Sense of Something Strange* (pp. 210-21). He substituted pseudonyms for the participants' names – except for himself and a co-investigator, the Rev. Max Magee. One might wonder why he bothered to change names that were already in the public domain, but at least he acknowledged that he was using pseudonyms. Regrettably, though, he didn't say that he'd also changed the name of the principal location, Balornock. His chapter on the case is misleadingly titled 'The House at Maxwell Park'. It may be that Roy alighted on this place name because his colleague was *Max Magee*. There is, in fact, a Maxwell Park in Glasgow. It's an actual park, not a housing scheme, and it's located on the south side of the city, in a salubrious district called Pollokshields (see photograph), which is very different from working-class Balornock on the north side of Glasgow. Maybe Roy didn't intend to deceive his readers – perhaps he simply forgot to say that he'd changed the name of the place. However, interviewed in 2008, he was still referring to it as Maxwell Park.[7] Even if he felt there was a legitimate reason not to mention Balornock, he could have simply referred to the location as Glasgow, or he could have refrained from giving any place name at all.

There's a reasonably clear and detailed account of the case in Geoff Holder's well-researched book *Poltergeist over Scotland* (pp. 158-66), which gives the true location of the principal events and the real names of the main participants.

**Street beside Maxwell Park in Pollokshields**

The case involved multiple witnesses. According to most sources, the phenomena began in early November 1974. However, the late James McHarg (1977), a psychiatrist with an interest in the paranormal, who visited the Grieves on three occasions, stated that the first manifestation was a loud bump, occurring about 11 p.m. one night in August or September 1974. It was reportedly followed, for about an hour, by further inexplicable noises. Eventually, there were other typical poltergeist phenomena, such as the displacement of household objects and electrical problems.

The disturbances weren't confined to Northgate Quadrant. For example, poltergeist activity followed the Grieves to the home of Mrs Grieve's sister and her husband, three-quarters of a mile away. One of the manifestations there entailed drops of water falling from the ceiling. However, when it was checked, the ceiling was found to be dry and free from any condensation.

Phenomena continued, intermittently, into the summer of 1975, or possibly a little later, finally ending after Derek Grieve, who was then 15, achieved his ambition of obtaining an apprenticeship as an electrician. He seems to have been the focus of much of the activity. It's worth noting that there was bad feeling between the Grieves and their downstairs neighbours, the Keenans, and that James Keenan died of lung cancer in May 1975.

## Recurrent manifestations associated with building renovations

Phenomena of the haunting or poltergeist type sometimes accompany, or closely follow, building renovation work. I'll cite two cases (for further examples, see McCue, 2010). The first one (Case 8) is quite strong, because several witnesses testified to experiencing phenomena. However, the apparent link with renovation work could be nothing more than a coincidence, since the premises concerned (a hotel) had a prior reputation for being haunted. In the second case, the link with renovation work seems more overt, although the case as a whole is weaker, because there was only one witness, and the person who has reported the story doesn't seem to have sought corroboration from anyone else.

*Case 8: Haunting*

Flitwick Manor in Bedfordshire was the ancestral home of the Brooks family for many years, but is now a hotel. In 1995, an attic room was discovered during renovation work on the roof. Three days later, a hotel guest called John Hinds checked out after a disturbed night. He'd apparently sensed a presence in his bedroom, and five minutes later it seemed that something heavy had landed at the foot of his bed, although he saw nothing to account for it when he turned on a light. A few minutes later, he heard shuffling at the bottom of the bed and then saw the silhouette of a person sitting there. The following night, hotel receptionist Lydia Dawson was in bed in the hotel when she saw a female apparition. She ran from the room without turning the lights on, but they were all on when she returned. The hotel manager, Sonia Banks, also had a strange experience. Staying alone in the hotel one night, in a room on the second floor, she heard footsteps going across the ceiling, and she heard a door slamming towards the front of the building, where the attic room had been discovered. And the head chef, Duncan Poyser, reported having had a strange experience while he was in bed in a room on the second floor. He tried to turn, but found himself temporarily unable to move his lower legs.

The case was featured in an episode of the ITV series *Strange but True?*, which dealt with paranormal experiences.[8] John Lyall, a descendent of the Brooks family, spent his childhood at the Manor. He appeared on the programme and related that when he was a child, his mother had spoken of hearing knocking sounds on her bedroom door while she was lying in bed. And he said that there'd been stories in the village about the house being haunted. Possibly, then, the renovation work reactivated a dormant haunting. I contacted the hotel in December 2008, and was informed that 'guests and staff are still experiencing strange phenomena'.

*Case 9: Haunting*

People of a spiritualist persuasion have proposed that in building renovation cases, the work may have offended the spirit of a former occupant of the property, who then shows his or her displeasure by producing paranormal manifestations. A dramatic case that seemingly fits this pattern has recently been cited by Cindy Parmiter.[9]

The alleged witness, Becky Parson, conveyed her story to Parmiter in late 2017. Becky, a city girl, had reportedly bought a small bungalow on the Virginia coast as a vacation home. The seller explained that the former owner was her aunt, who'd recently died after spending several months in a nursing facility.

Becky took some time off work to oversee renovations at the building. She'd decided to hire contractors to remove a wall that separated the kitchen from the living area. A fresh layer of paint and some minor repair work would complete the job. Everything went to plan on the first day. But as she lay in bed that night, she began to sense that something wasn't right. Sometime before dawn, she was allegedly awakened by a pounding sound from the living room area. By the time that she got dressed, things had gone silent, and when she stepped out of the bedroom, she saw that there were no lights on in the bungalow. A little later, as she sat at the breakfast nook, drinking coffee, she experienced a sinking feeling in the pit of her stomach; and as she gazed out of the window, she felt anger and sadness welling up inside her for no reason.

When the workers arrived, hours later, Becky was still sitting by the window. A crushing sense of depression had come over her, making it nearly impossible for her to move. When she realized that she was in the way, she managed to take herself to the bedroom, where she sat on the bed and wept. Throughout the day, her emotions swung back and forth from boiling anger to devastating sorrow.

The contractor told Becky that they would be back in the morning to complete the job. Before leaving, he explained that they'd left the windows open to let the paint fumes escape. He wanted to make sure that she secured the bungalow before nightfall. Overall, she was thrilled with how the restructuring had gone, but she couldn't help feeling that something was wrong. She found that she had little appetite for her supper. After tidying up, she went for a bath. She'd just settled into the tub when a series of loud bangs came from the living room. When she checked, she discovered that the windows, left open by the renovation workers, were now closed, although there were no signs of an intruder.

That night, Becky examined some photographs, emailed to her by the contractor, showing 'before' and 'after' pictures relating to the renovation work. Eventually, she noticed something vague, resembling a patch of fog, in each of the photographs taken after the renovations had begun. There was no such effect in any of the 'before' snaps.

In bed, Becky tossed and turned most of that night; and, at some point, she heard the sound of footsteps just outside the bedroom. But she feared that if she got up and confronted the intruder, it wouldn't end well for her. The footfalls became more and more frenzied and seemed to be getting closer to the bedroom. After several minutes, the pacing came to a halt in the doorway of the room, and she felt as if eyes were boring into her. Then, a male voice unleashed a torrent of hateful words at her, saying that he'd warned her that this would happen and that she should have listened. He also said that she'd always thought that she knew it all. Interestingly, though, Becky had the impression that this tirade wasn't really aimed at her, but at someone with whom the speaker had had a personal connection. The house eventually fell silent. However, this was only the first of many such 'visits', which could occur at any time of day or night.

Becky hoped that things would go back to normal after the completion of the renovation work. But, if anything, incidents became more frequent, and she eventually packed up her things and returned to the city. After a while, she phoned the woman who'd sold her the beach house, and Becky ended up relating her experiences.

Becky knew that the seller's aunt had lived in the house for decades before her death. Becky asked whether the aunt had ever mentioned having any similar experiences. The seller explained that she and her aunt hadn't been close and that she (the seller) hadn't been told of anything. However, she added that if the house was indeed haunted by an angry spirit, she had an idea as to its identity. She was referring to her late uncle, who'd died several years before her aunt. Apparently, he'd been a difficult person to get on with, putting it mildly, and ruled his home with an iron fist, dominating his wife, who wasn't allowed to do things without his permission.

According to Parmiter's article, Becky was satisfied that she'd unravelled the mystery of the beach house, but she was holding onto the property for the time being. She planned to restore it to its former self as soon as she could afford to. For reasons that she couldn't fully explain, she felt a connection with it, despite her encounters with the supposed spirit. She hoped that the entity would be appeased once everything had been returned to its original state and that she would finally be able to enjoy her holiday home. Parmiter noted that Becky was still paying occasional visits to the property, although she seldom stayed overnight.

I'm not personally acquainted with Becky or with Cindy Parmiter, and I can't vouch for the accuracy of this story. Given the intensity of the alleged phenomena and the fact that she was supposedly there on her own, I find it a little hard to believe that Becky remained in the beach house as long as she reportedly did. Assuming that the story isn't a fabrication, three rather different possibilities come to mind. (1) The phenomena may indeed have been generated by the 'earthbound spirit' of the aforementioned man. (2) To some extent, Becky had tapped into the thoughts and feelings that previous occupants had once had there, which perhaps implies that some sort of 'recording' and 'replaying' mechanism was at work, although that wouldn't explain the physical phenomena (windows being slammed shut, and photographic anomalies). (3) The phenomena were the orchestrations of a tricksterish higher intelligence that, among other things, likes to fabricate evidence suggestive of spirit activity.

# CHAPTER 4

# PARANORMAL VENDETTAS

This chapter looks at cases in which people seem to have been the victims of paranormal persecution. In a broad sense of the term, at least, the victims seem to have come under a curse. As will be seen, in respect of Case 1, there may well have been an explicit cursing ritual. It's not clear whether that was so in Case 2, although there is no doubt that hostile feelings were directed towards the victims (or, at least, one of them) and their home. In terms of the distinction made in Chapter 1, these cases exemplify Type I curses. That is, the victims were plagued by phenomena of an overtly paranormal nature (poltergeist-type manifestations). If the reported details can be believed, Case 3 involved paranormal phenomena and also 'bad luck' (the latter being a defining feature of Type II curses). If the events occurred as described, it may have been non-human entities that pursued the vendetta. In Case 4, the source of the persecutory activity may have been the vengeful spirit of a man who'd committed suicide, although other interpretations are possible. This could be classed as another Type I case, since the manifestations entailed violent poltergeist-type disturbances. In Case 5, the victim got a fright. But, for her, it seems to have been a one-off experience rather than a vendetta as such.

## CASE 1: THE DRUMMER OF TEDWORTH

This is a classic case from 17th-century England. Around the time, it was discussed, in print, by the Reverend Joseph Glanvill (1636-80). Detailed accounts of it can be found in the late Harry Price's book *Poltergeist* (1993, pp. 43-61; 388-99). Price quotes extensively from both Glanvill (who witnessed some of the phenomena) and one of the principal witnesses, John Mompesson (see below). The case is also covered in Sacheverell Sitwell's book *Poltergeists* (Sitwell, 1988, pp. 112-24; 134; 214-29; 304).

However, given the archaic language in which the events are described, and because of historical uncertainties, this isn't the easiest of cases to get a handle on. I'll attempt no more than giving an outline, citing a few examples of the reported phenomena, and offering some comments.

The principal events occurred at the home of John Mompesson, a socially well-connected magistrate, who lived with his wife, children, mother, and servants in the Manor House at North Tedworth (now known as North Tidworth) in Wiltshire. Glanvill placed the occurrences between April 1661 and January 1663, but it seems that they actually spanned the period March 1662 to April 1663 (Price, 1993, p. 388). However, although the events leading up to the disturbances may have begun in March 1662, the paranormal phenomena seem to have begun a little later.

One day in mid-March 1662, while Mompesson was at the house of the bailiff of Ludgershall, Wiltshire, he heard drum beats. The bailiff explained that, for some days, they'd been bothered by a drummer who was asking the local constable for money on the basis of a document that he (the drummer) possessed, although the bailiff thought it was bogus. Mompesson sent the constable to bring the man, William Drury, to the bailiff's house for questioning. Drury's document was supposedly endorsed by two people whom Mompesson happened to know, and Mompesson discerned that it was indeed counterfeit. He instructed that Drury's drum be taken from him and that he be scheduled for an appearance before a justice of the peace. Drury then confessed his misdemeanour and pleaded to be given back his drum. He claimed a connection with a Colonel Ayliff (one of the people who'd supposedly endorsed the bogus document). Mompesson told Drury that he'd check with Ayliff, and if the latter reported that Drury had been an honest man, he'd get his drum back, although it would be withheld in the meantime. Mompesson left the drum with the bailiff, and Drury with the constable. But it seems that in response to pleadings from Drury, the constable let him go.

## Poltergeist phenomena at Mompesson's home

The next month (April), the bailiff sent the confiscated drum to Mompesson's house (quite why isn't clear to me). At the time, Mompesson was preparing for a journey to London. When he returned from the trip, on 4 May, his pregnant wife explained that the family had been disturbed by nocturnal noises, which she attributed to thieves. A few nights later, Mompesson had his first taste of the phenomena. In a letter to an acquaintance, the Rev. William Creed, D.D. (reproduced in Appendix A of Price's book), Mompesson stated that, as he went up and down the house armed with pistols, he heard 'a strange noise and hollow sound', but couldn't see anything unusual. And 'then it came oftener, five nights, and absent three [...] and thump very hard, all in ye outside of my house, and constantly came when we were going to sleep, whether early or late' (quoted by Price, *ibid.*, p. 395).

Of course, regarding noises seemingly coming from outside the house, one might wonder whether pranksters (possibly associated with, or including, Drury) were sneaking around, banging on the building.[1] However, in his letter to Dr Creed, Mompesson noted that after a month, auditory phenomena occurred *within* the room containing the drum.

Throughout the disturbances, many other phenomena were witnessed inside the house. For example, in his letter to Creed, Mompesson refers to an occasion when chairs walked about a room by themselves, children's shoes were hurled over the witnesses' heads and every loose thing moved about the chamber. Judging from Glanvill's account in Price's book, there were also visual manifestations. For instance, there was an occasion when Mompesson's 'Man' (personal servant?) saw a figure standing at the foot of his bed. He couldn't discern its exact shape, but it had a large body and red, glaring eyes, which stared at him intently for a while, after which the figure disappeared. Glanvill also recounts an occasion, about the beginning of April 1663, when Mompesson went into his stable and saw a strange sight. The horse he was accustomed to riding was lying on the ground, with one of its hind legs stuck in its mouth. It was difficult for several men to lever it out.

## More on William Drury

Drury had apparently spent four years in the Parliamentary army (around the time of the Civil War, I presume). Thereafter, he worked briefly at his trade as a tailor. Then, according to Mompesson's letter to William Creed, Drury 'went upp and down ye Countrey to show Hocas pocus, feates of activity, dancing through hoops and such like devices' (quoted by Price, *ibid.*, p. 397).

From what's in Price's book, I'm a bit confused about the precise history of Drury's brushes with the law, and I can't guarantee that the following details are entirely accurate and complete. For one thing, I don't know whether he was ever prosecuted over the matter of the forged document. At some point, he wound up in prison at Gloucester, apparently for stealing pigs. While there, he reportedly boasted of being behind Mompesson's troubles, and when he heard of this, Mompesson sought to have Drury tried for witchcraft. Glanvill (quoted by Price, *ibid.*, p. 56) noted that Drury claimed to have books by someone regarded as a wizard. The case was heard at Salisbury, and although Drury was acquitted of witchcraft, he was sentenced to transportation to one of Britain's colonies (Virginia), maybe because he was deemed to be a rogue and a vagabond. However, he somehow managed to 'escape', although I'm not sure whether that means that he broke free of custody (in which case he would have presumably been at risk of re-arrest) or whether the transportation order somehow became null and void. According to a footnote on p. 61 of Price's book, the subsequent history of Drury isn't well known; but Price says that it's pretty certain that he fell into the hands of the police, and that maybe a second attempt to transport him was successful.

## Comments

Evidentially, this case seems fairly strong. There were multiple witnesses, and we have first-hand testimony from a principal witness, John Mompesson, in the form of his letter to Dr Creed. (The version reproduced by Price in his book is based on a copy he obtained, not the original.) Additionally, on an unnumbered page facing p. 52 of his book, Price has reproduced handwritten diary extracts from Mompesson, which mention manifestations. And, as noted, Joseph Glanvill reported having witnessed some of the phenomena.

It's worth noting that the phenomena began soon after Drury's drum was sent to Mompesson's house. Maybe it acted as a 'cursed object' (i.e. as a 'carrier' or facilitator of Drury's presumed curse). It's perhaps surprising that Mompesson didn't arrange for it to be sent elsewhere. Further cases of 'cursed objects' are discussed in the next chapter.

Mompesson had quite a few children. To some extent, the phenomena focused on them, or some of them. Their presence may have acted as a catalyst for the manifestations. Interestingly, though, there was little noise on the night when Mompesson's wife was in labour with their latest child, and none for the following three weeks. Was the intelligence behind the phenomena being considerate, or was this simply a matter of chance?

In this case, it may not have been William Drury himself who brought about the poltergeist phenomena, but some sort of mischievous intelligence that stepped in to assist him! I'll return to this notion in Chapter 9.

## CASE 2: STONED IN SOUTH LONDON

I mentioned the late Mary Rose Barrington in the previous chapter. Her 2019 book *Talking about Psychical Research* includes a chapter titled 'Can Hatred Throw Stones?' (pp. 25-31). It describes an intriguing, long-running poltergeist case from south London. The page numbers cited below refer to the book. Barrington doesn't specify the precise location of the afflicted house, and I don't know it myself. She's used pseudonyms for the people concerned, which I'll also use. I don't know their real names.

**The key players**

Before detailing the reported events, it may help if I say a few words about the main participants.

Carol Finn was in her mid-forties when the activity began, in 1986. Barrington described her as being 'a totally outgoing, frank and friendly personality, radiating common sense, responsibility and self-confidence, with [a] good sense of humour, seemingly devoid, so far as is humanly possible, of hang-ups' (p. 26). She was generally, but not always, at work when things happened. Barrington doesn't say what her occupation was.

Carol's mother, who died in 1997, lived with Carol, as did Malcolm, Carol's younger brother, who worked as a decorator. Barrington describes him as being very good-natured, polite, and devoted to an extremely old dog, just one of a large number of pets sharing the house with the adults.

Muriel was Carol's younger sister. She and her husband, a builder, lived about five miles away in rented accommodation. They had a son (Gary) and a daughter. Muriel got on better with her daughter than with Gary, and it seems that he and his sister didn't get along well. From when he was 16, Gary had spent most of his time at Carol's home; and when he was 19, he went to live there, whereupon Carol started sharing a bedroom with her mother. That meant that Gary could take over her former bedroom.

## Resentment

The phenomena described below occurred in an interesting psychological context. Barrington explains that:

> In the early 1970s, before the start of mega property-price inflation, Carol decided to put her savings into house purchase, and, as her mother was to live in the house too, mother contributed her small amount of capital. That house was sold at a profit and, in 1976, Carol bought the house where she still lived [...]. Muriel [and her husband] continued to rent. Muriel expressed some considerable resentment that her mother had 'favoured' Carol by contributing money to her house purchase, and the fact that their mother was also to live there did not, in Muriel's eyes, justify this subsidy to Carol, though at the time it was a relatively small sore point.
>
> But we know what has happened to houses in the London area; over twenty-five years they rocketed in value and become worth about 100 times more than their purchase price, while people who rent have to pay ever more to keep up with the increased freehold values. Muriel's small sore point inflated at about the same rate as the property market, and became a matter of barely contained envy and resentment. The key incident about to be related describes an occasion when the venom was not contained.
>
> Carol had reluctantly complied with her mother's wish to invite Muriel and her husband to lunch. One o'clock came, 2 o'clock, and near to 3 o'clock they arrived, angrily complaining about traffic, though not actually apologising for coming very late indeed. Carol handed out glasses of wine, but found it difficult to make polite conversation. Muriel asked somewhat aggressively what was the matter with her, to which Carol replied that she was rather hungry after the long wait.
>
> Muriel responded by doing two things: first, she threw her glass of wine at Carol, who put up a hand to protect her face; whereupon a shard of glass embedded itself in her hand with such vigour that instead of having lunch she had to be taken to the hospital for stitches. As a mere aside, I consider it strange that the glass should

have shattered either in mid-air or on contact with the palm of a hand, and, if it was broken before being thrown, you might have expected Muriel to suffer injury – but let us leave that hanging in the air. It is the words that accompanied the flung wine glass that are really significant. Out of a conversational vacuum Muriel shouted with superb irrelevance: 'And you can keep your bloody house!' No one had mentioned the house, least of all Carol, who had said only that she was hungry; so it is likely enough that Muriel and her husband must have been having a smouldering conversation on this subject as they finally drove up to it. The throwing of the wineglass, with sufficient violence to injure Carol, and the bitter words about the house, all point to a festering resentment directed at Carol, but embracing her mother, Malcolm and, incidentally, the dogs, who have also been the victims of thrown objects and even more peculiar things. The Finn poltergeist was definitely more malicious than playful. [pp. 27-8]

Furthermore, Barrington notes:

That the unloved Gary should have moved into Carol's house must surely have been a further irritant for Muriel – a silent reproach that she, his mother, had not wanted him while Carol, merely his aunt, had taken him in, and given him her room, and her TV, and given him the shelter and comfort that he would have expected to get from his own parents. [p. 29]

Unfortunately, Barrington doesn't give a date for the occasion when Muriel threw a wine glass at Carol, although she explains that, by then, Gary was spending most of his time staying with his girlfriend.

**The phenomena**

As I've already noted, the manifestations began in 1986. It was nearly 10 years after Carol purchased the house, and not long after her nephew Gary moved in. By the time that members of the SPR got to know about it, the house 'had been subjected to almost daily stoning for more than three years and all the windows were covered with chicken wire to protect them from the large stones that struck the exterior on most days and nights' (pp. 25-6). Barrington saw a large file of correspondence between Carol and the local police, whom she (Carol) severely castigated for failing to catch the presumed vandals.

Barrington noted that before the stoning, there'd been a sort of prelude. Malcolm had painted the outside window frames and the front door; and the next day, it was found that ripe blackberries had been thrown at the paintwork, staining it with unsightly purple blotches. But Barrington wasn't convinced that this particular piece of vandalism was paranormal. She wrote:

> ...Incredible to relate, Muriel's husband had a rather juvenile and dangerous hobby of projecting objects from a large catapult and [that] may have been the precipitating factor behind the paranormal stoning. [...] It could be that in poltergeist cases paranormal action mimics and builds on normal action that a hostile personality sets in motion. [pp. 29-30]

It's not clear from Barrington's chapter whether the stoning began immediately after this 'prelude', or after a gap of time. At any rate, Gary was with Malcolm when it began. A stone came through the kitchen window. They rushed to look through it, to see who might be responsible.

Barrington explains:

> ...The only vantage point from which it could reasonably have been projected was their own garden, and there was no one there. I say 'reasonably' because the garden that backed on to theirs would be a considerable distance away from the window.
>
> As it happens, the owner of that garden was standing close to the boundary fence, looking towards Carol's house, and looking very startled. They looked at him and found that he was looking at them. That is a strange thing for the neighbour to do if, for some unknown reason, he had hurled the stone – you would expect him to be pretending to weed the lawn, or something like that – but it is consistent with his seeing a stone flying through the air and wondering where it came from. As it happens, the man died a few weeks later, but the stone-throwing burgeoned. [p. 29]

Of course, it might be surmised that Muriel's husband, possibly aided by accomplices, was somehow avoiding detection by the police and regularly pelting the house with stones. But after Maurice Grosse, one of the first SPR investigators on the scene, suggested to Carol that paranormal activity might be occurring, the stone-throwing became intermittent, and phenomena began to take place *inside* the house, for which Carol's brother-in-law couldn't have been responsible. However, Barrington explains that nothing happened when investigators were present:

> ...I was frequently there to witness scenes of devastation: a flood that had no ascertainable cause, glass embedded in the wall from bottles of milk flung across the room, an upturned pot of paint in the refrigerator, and so on. But every resident could be exonerated from several of the main incidents, and I see no room to doubt that the phenomena were paranormal. If (as I suspect) the primary motivation behind the poltergeistery was to make the house look very unattractive outside and uncomfortable inside, that object was well and truly achieved, with its conservatory boarded up and front door daubed from time to time. [p. 26]

Barrington reflects on possible links between tensions within Carol's household and the phenomena. Regarding Carol's mother, she notes:

> ...Even if Carol was her preferred daughter, it was disturbing to have another daughter so deeply antagonistic. Moreover it was my impression that [the mother] was not entirely pleased at having Gary around, and not at all happy about having him living in the house. She had been fond of him when he was a boy, but boys can become yobbish young men, and, as she made clear to me, she was afraid of his fixation on strength, power and muscle. And it was not only Carol who sacrificed a bedroom of her own – her mother had to share hers with Carol. I don't suppose she liked that at all, but probably felt that it would be selfish and ungrandmotherly to refuse to fall in with Carol's willingness to rough it. I have no doubt that she was highly relieved when, in 1993, Gary finally went off and moved in with his girlfriend. His departure marked a steady decline in manifestations, which ceased altogether with the death of Carol's mother in 1997. [p. 30]

But Barrington didn't believe that the mother was faking manifestations:

> ...[Don't] imagine that [she] sneaked down in the middle of the night and spent several hours standing on chairs decorating the kitchen ceiling with intricate patterns composed of Branston pickle, because I'm sure she could not and did not. For one thing, at the time of this event she was sharing her bedroom with Carol, and both she and the dogs would have noticed her, or anyone else, going downstairs and beavering away in the middle of the night at a rather noisy, dirty and smelly activity. I am equally sure that she didn't unscrew light bulbs from the chandelier and throw them around. [p. 27]

Equally, Barrington notes that Gary had to be eliminated from fabricating many of the incidents:

> ...Carol's mother described to me how she, Malcolm and Gary had been peaceably sitting in the living room in full view of one another (Carol was at work) when some milk bottles that had been in the hall were flung from the hall across the room. Carol's mother recalled, with something of a shudder, how excited Gary had been by the display of force. I see Gary not as a perpetrator but as a sort of psychometric object, an aerial or perhaps a tuned circuit, facilitating reception of his mother's malice towards the house and its people. [p. 29]

**Comments**

It would be interesting to know whether Muriel and her husband had any interest in, or knowledge of, the occult. But Barrington evidently doubted whether they employed an explicit cursing ritual:

> My conclusion is that Muriel's hatred, her husband's catapulting and Gary's love of power displays could have been the constituents of the powerhouse that gave rise to the paranormal action, shaped and sustained it. In some societies, regarded in un-PC terms as backward, a man who falls ill asks 'Who is doing this to me?' the assumption being that someone is sticking pins in his image or burning a hair from his head. I don't see Muriel and her family attempting some Hammer horror technique, because it would never occur to them that

it might work, but I can imagine their subconscious getting up to all sorts of horrible things. [pp. 30-1]

So far as I know, Barrington never met or communicated with Muriel and her husband. Therefore, her assumption that the idea of a cursing ritual wouldn't have occurred to them seems a little presumptuous.

Although it's tempting to infer that the long-running poltergeist phenomena at Carol's home were related to her sister and brother-in-law's negative feelings, we can't, of course, be sure that that was the case. Maybe the phenomena would have occurred even if Muriel and her husband had been well disposed towards Carol.

## CASE 3: MISFORTUNE BEFALLING UFO RESEARCHERS

After UFO sightings, witnesses are sometimes unable to account for a period of time (a phenomenon often referred to as 'missing time' or what might be better called 'paranormal amnesia'). They might be troubled by vague feelings, flashbacks, and partial recollections. They might spot marks or scars that they hadn't noticed before, or they might become aware of small foreign objects ('implants') within their bodies. Over time, and perhaps with the aid of hypnotic regression, they might recall abduction scenarios involving otherworldly entities.[2] Alien abduction (however we interpret it) seems to be a recurrent experience for some people, and it's typically a source of considerable distress. In some cases, different generations within a family are seemingly targeted.

The nature of alien abduction experiences has been a focus of debate and controversy. Some commentators incline to the view that the recollections of supposed abductees are fantasies (see, for example, Watson, 2009), while others believe that they are indicative of genuine contact with extraterrestrial or other-dimensional entities (see, for example, Hopkins, 1983; Jacobs, 1999; Mack, 1995). Accounts often feature medical examinations and reproductive procedures. Indeed, some researchers believe that aliens are systematically engaged in creating human-alien hybrids, and using human female abductees as incubators.

Paul Sinclair is based in Bridlington, East Yorkshire. He's the author of three books about anomalous phenomena that he's investigated in and around his home area (*Truth-Proof*, *Truth-Proof 2*, and *Truth-Proof 3*). In passing, they mention unusual phenomena that he's experienced himself. His latest (2020) book, *Night People*, is much more personal, providing detailed, gripping, and disturbing accounts of strange incidents going back to his early childhood. In many respects, his story is typical of someone who's been a victim of the alien abduction phenomenon (however one interprets it). But sensibly, in my view, he's open-minded about the source of the intrusions. He doesn't, for instance, insist that the entities he's encountered have been extraterrestrial.

Sinclair's early life wasn't easy. His parents weren't the type to listen sympathetically to a traumatized young child describing strange night intruders, and he realized that. His fear of the 'visitors' got to the point where, at night, he remained in bed rather than get up to visit the lavatory if needed. Consequently, he developed a problem with bedwetting, for which he would be slapped by his father. He explains that his wife and other family members have had entity encounters. For example, in 2017, he learned that a grandson was reporting incidents in which a hole would open in a wall in his bedroom, with a thin blue man then coming out of it and crawling up the bed. In line with other accounts, the book cites physical evidence. For example, after a night in which Sinclair recalls aliens performing a painful procedure on his back, he woke with punched-out holes behind his right shoulder blade. Interestingly, though, there wasn't a mark on the white shirt he'd been wearing the night before. Furthermore, a neighbour from across the road reportedly saw three huge flashes of blue light coming from the Sinclairs' house just after 3 a.m. on the night in question.

## Philip Imbrogno's story

In his book *Interdimensional Universe*, USA-based Philip Imbrogno (2008, pp. 198-216) describes a series of strange events that allegedly began in February 1978 after he received a call from a single mother whom he calls Sandra (pseudonym).

Sandra reportedly claimed that she, her mother, and her daughter had had many UFO experiences, and that alien-like beings had often walked into their home through the walls, via a black rotating hole, and had taken them away to somewhere they couldn't remember. This had been occurring, it appeared, since her mother was nine years old; and Sandra recalled having gone through the 'black hole' herself at times when she was a child. She explained that these intrusions had stopped for many years, but had then started up again, with her daughter being the focus of attention.

Imbrogno states that he visited Sandra's home with some fellow investigators. They reportedly witnessed an unusual event outside the house, involving a globe of yellow light, about six inches in diameter, which moved across the front lawn, some 10 feet above the ground. When Imbrogno got to within about 20 feet of it, a tingling sensation went up and down his neck. Then, after stopping in mid-air, as if to observe him, the light shot straight up into the sky.

The following month, Imbrogno returned to Sandra's home with a psychologist who had a background in hypnotic regression. Under hypnosis, Sandra recalled experiences of the UFO/entity encounter type. Her daughter was ill with the flu at the time and was sleeping in her bedroom. However, just after Sandra came out of hypnosis, her daughter started screaming and jumped out of bed. She claimed that the 'man from the hole' had come and had said that he was going to take her. Asked what else he'd said, she explained that he'd threatened to 'get' Imbrogno and his friends if they didn't leave the entities alone.

Imbrogno had tape-recorded the hypnosis session. When he and the other team members listened to the recording, they reportedly heard strange noises throughout most of it. But at one point, a very audible voice uttered a threat. Imbrogno took the tape to a friend who did audio recordings for a university. When it was played backwards, a voice could be heard. It claimed to be that of an entity from a place that's parallel with our world. Among other things, it threatened that if the investigators continued to interfere with the entities' work, they would have no choice but to take action against the investigators.

Shortly after that, a fellow team member told Imbrogno that he was hearing voices; and the next day, he reported that entities had appeared in his bedroom. Not long after, Imbrogno heard that this colleague had been killed by jumping in front of a train! Another team member, Frank, left the group after being visited by someone claiming to be from the National Security Agency and who reportedly told Frank that he would lose his commercial pilot's licence if he continued with UFO investigations. A third team member, Carl, told Imbrogno about a 'dream', which he'd had the night before, in which he'd awoken to see a tall, hooded figure that stretched out a hand on which there was a beating heart. The entity reportedly said, 'This could be your heart', and then squeezed the organ, bursting it. Carl then awoke in a cold sweat. He subsequently died from heart failure after an operation to correct a recently discovered valve defect. Apart from Imbrogno, that left just two team members. One of them, a police officer, dropped out of UFO research after he and his wife had a number of sightings that terrified them both, although Imbrogno doesn't specify what these alleged sightings entailed. The other team member, an engineer, continued for a year or so, keeping mainly to himself. In 1979 or 1980, he told Imbrogno that he was giving up UFO research. Imbrogno notes that the colleague was beginning to live his life in fear, because so many bizarre things had seemingly happened to him.

Imbrogno mentions the occupations of his fellow team members, but not their surnames. Accordingly, they're effectively anonymous. The story might strain people's credulity, because UFO investigators don't normally experience such dramatic events (e.g. colleagues dying in strange circumstances).

Some years ago, Imbrogno's credentials (e.g. his supposedly having degrees from the prestigious Massachusetts Institute of Technology) were called into question, and he seems to have withdrawn from the field of paranormal research.[3] But if he misrepresented aspects of his background, it doesn't necessarily follow that he lied about the UFO and paranormal cases that he wrote about.

## CASE 4: INDRIDI INDRIDASON

Spiritualists believe that we are essentially spiritual beings, and that our spirits survive physical death and can communicate with those still in the flesh. Spiritualist mediums act as channels through which spirits of the dead supposedly communicate with the living. The majority of mediums are described as *mental mediums*, to distinguish them from *physical mediums*, who manifest phenomena such as object movements and materializations.

The majority of mental mediums seem to remain in a normal state of consciousness when conveying supposed messages from the dead. The scene is reminiscent of someone speaking on a phone and intermittently breaking off to address bystanders. But mediums' pronouncements are often impressionistic remarks rather than clear-cut messages ('I'm seeing a lady in a blue dress...I think she passed over sometime last year...I'm getting the name June or Judy...').

Some mental mediums go into a trance (or, at least, give the impression of doing so), whereupon a 'control' (supposedly a minder from the spirit world) takes over and speaks to the sitters, acting as an intermediary between them and the presumed communicating spirits. The 'control' might have an exotic name. Speaking through the medium's vocal cords, he or she will typically have a different accent from the medium's normal one, and the performance might have a decidedly theatrical quality. There are at least three possibilities regarding the nature of these 'controls': (1) the medium is deliberately putting on a theatrical performance; (2) the 'control' is a secondary personality of the medium; (3) the 'control' is indeed an external intelligence from the 'spirit world' or elsewhere.

It would be beyond the scope of this book to go into details here, but research evidence indicates that the statements of mental mediums are sometimes significantly more accurate than one would expect from intelligent guesswork (see, for example, Fontana, 2005). For example, if a medium purports to be in touch with your deceased grandmother, surprisingly accurate information about her might come through. This could be interpreted as evidence of spirit communication, although another possibility is that, unconsciously, the medium has read your mind, telepathically, or has gleaned the information from elsewhere by ESP.

Physical mediums are rare. If they prefer their séances to be conducted in private, with regular sitters, it may be difficult for outsiders to get an opportunity to see them in action. They typically go into a trance (or give an appearance of doing so), whereupon a 'control' personality takes over. Thereafter, physical phenomena might ensue. A semi-physical material known as ectoplasm is supposedly released by physical mediums during séances, enabling the presumed spirits to create temporary materializations and physical effects.

Physical mediums generally work in conditions of darkness or very limited light. It's claimed that if light were suddenly introduced into the proceedings, the ectoplasm would recoil violently into the medium's body, leading to serious injury. But, of course, the need for darkness creates conditions in which deception can occur; and many fraudulent mediums have been detected by alert investigators. Among other ruses, cheesecloth has been used to mimic ectoplasm, dolls have been used to represent spirits, and rods have been employed to move objects. Of course, hard-line sceptics might suggest that *all* physical mediumship is a 'con'. But such a global dismissal seems unjustified. Take, for example, the Scottish-born medium Daniel Dunglas Home (1833-1886). He produced a wide range of physical manifestations, such as levitation of his own body, levitation of furniture, materializations, luminous appearances, and percussive sounds.[4] Many of the phenomena were apparently produced in good light, and he was never caught faking manifestations.

There's a thin line between poltergeist phenomena and the effects produced by physical mediums. In the case of the latter, the manifestations are generally controlled and not destructive. However, there are reports of things getting out of hand, as a story concerning an Icelandic physical medium illustrates.

Indridi Indridason (1883-1912) grew up on a farm in north-western Iceland. At the age of 22, he moved to Reykjavik and became an apprentice printer. Eventually, he started taking part in meetings of a spiritualist group and soon displayed phenomena of the type associated with mediums such as D. D. Home. Like Home, he died of tuberculosis.

Fontana (2005, pp. 287-94) and Erlendur Haraldsson[5] discuss violent disturbances witnessed in connection with Indridason's mediumship. At some point in 1907, Indridason reportedly perceived, clairvoyantly, the figure of someone who, unbeknown to him, had recently committed suicide. The medium made some mocking remarks about this person, who appears to have been a Jon Einarsson. Shortly after, during a séance, Indridason's spirit 'controls' said that 'Jon' was present and in control of the 'power' and that they didn't know how the séance would end. Sitters' chairs were reportedly thrown around the room, the medium was tipped out of his chair, a scuttle full of coal was thrown at a spot where someone had been standing a moment before, and unseen hands clutched the clothes of sitters. The séances were temporarily discontinued, but there were then disturbances in the medium's living quarters. He was so alarmed by this that two companions, by the name of Oddgeirsson and Kvaran, stayed with him overnight. The three of them then fled to Kvaran's house, but violent disturbances continued there for some nights. Séances were eventually resumed after it seemed that the medium's spirit 'controls' had managed to drive out 'Jon'. However, 'he' then spoke through an 'independent voice' (I presume this means not through Indridason) and further violent disturbances ensued, such as heavy objects being thrown about and smashed, and 'Jon' shouting and abusing people through a trumpet flying around the room. It seems that during further séances, more than one 'hostile spirit' was present, although violent activity largely ceased.

## CASE 5: A FRIGHTENING SENSE OF PRESENCE

In their book *Contagion*, Darren Ritson and Michael Hallowell (2014) discuss how poltergeist phenomena can spread out from the home of the principal witnesses and affect others, such as members of their extended family, or investigators. Ritson and Hallowell refer to this as *contagion* (hence the title of their book). Subjects of contagion typically find their experiences perplexing and frightening, but Ritson and Hallowell note that, as it spreads, the activity seems to become diluted (p. 16). They speculate that contagion can be either 'active' or 'passive' (pp. 31-2). With the former, someone (or perhaps more than one person) connected with the afflicted person or family would be deliberately targeted by the intelligence behind the phenomena. In passive contagion, however, the process would occur automatically. An analogy would be that of someone being accidentally infected with the common cold virus. Active (deliberate) contagion may not be sufficiently intense and long-lasting to warrant the label 'vendetta', but it may reflect negativity or hostility on the part of the intelligence behind the phenomena.

Ritson and Hallowell believe that there were numerous instances of contagion during their investigation of a major poltergeist case at South Shields in the north-east of England. For example, a respected graphologist, to whom they'd sent samples of ostensible poltergeist writing for analysis, was looking over the material in the garden of her London home when she suddenly felt a 'presence' behind her. She could 'sense' that it was a tall man in a long, dark coat. This matched the description given by a child at the South Shields home, who'd reportedly seen such a figure numerous times. The graphologist found the incident deeply disturbing (*ibid.*, p. 30).

# CHAPTER 5

# CURSED OBJECTS AND MATERIALS

This chapter looks at cases suggesting that physical objects (e.g. items of furniture) and materials (e.g. lava rock) may act as carriers or vectors for negative paranormal influences. If the reports can be believed, we could, perhaps, describe these objects and materials as 'cursed'.

However, to place things in a broader context, it's worth noting that some objects are believed, rightly or wrongly, to ward off evil, or even to bring good luck. It's also claimed that psychically gifted people may be able to pick up impressions about the history of objects or their owners by handling the items, a process known as 'object reading' or 'psychometry'. For instance, some years ago, I was talking to a man who seemed to have had various psychic experiences. I handed him my wrist-watch and asked him to tell me what impressions came to his mind. He said one or two things that I wouldn't have expected him to know about me, although it's possible that this related to lucky guesswork rather than ESP. But judging from reports, some gifted psychics have displayed truly remarkable object reading skills – for example, Alexis Didier (1826-86) and Stefan Ossowiecki (1877-1944), whose psychic abilities are discussed by Barrington (2019).

When someone displays object reading skills, it may be wrong to think that the information is drawn from the item itself. It may function merely as a psychological prop, enabling the person to exercise his or her powers of ESP.

In his book *Cursed Objects*, J. W. Ocker cites numerous tales of supposedly cursed items. He approaches the subject with a wry sense of humour, and my impression is that he regards the stories – or most of them, at least – as legends of folkloric interest rather than as rock-solid historical accounts of objects that are, or were, definitely cursed. Later in this chapter, I'll cite a few of the cases he mentions (Cases 8-12).

## CASE 1: THE HEXHAM HEADS

Several decades ago, intriguing events reportedly occurred in Hexham, a picturesque town in Northumberland, which is England's northernmost county. Related events subsequently occurred in Southampton, on the country's south coast. Unfortunately, regarding aspects of the case, there are conflicting versions of what happened. Author and journalist Paul Screeton hails from Hartlepool in the north-east of England. He has had a longstanding interest in this case, which he examines in detail in his 2012 book *Quest for the Hexham Heads*.[1] It's my principal source for what follows, although I don't find it a very lucid book. It doesn't, for example, present a clear timeline of the alleged events, and there's no index. But before I delve into some of the details, it may help if I give a brief overview of what supposedly happened.

### Overview

In 1971, two children (brothers Colin and Leslie Robson) found what appeared to be two small, stone heads in the garden of their semi-detached house at 3 Rede Avenue in Hexham. The items have come to be known as the 'Hexham Heads'. Shortly after their discovery, members of the Dodd family at the adjoining house (1 Rede Avenue) experienced strange events. Soon after, there were also manifestations at the boys' own home. Sometime later, the Hexham Heads fell into the temporary custody of Dr Anne Ross, an archaeologist and Celtic scholar. While the items were at her home in Southampton, paranormal phenomena occurred there. Indeed, they may have continued there even after the Heads were removed from the premises. Initially, at least, Ross was inclined to believe that the Hexham Heads were of ancient origin. But a former resident of the Robsons' house, Des Craigie, claimed that he'd made them from building materials in the 1950s. Over the years, the Heads were passed from person to person. But Paul Screeton doesn't know their current whereabouts.

**Rede Avenue, Hexham**

Given the conflicting testimony, I can't guarantee that the following details are all historically correct. In summarizing the case on the basis of Screeton's book, I've been selective, but hopefully balanced. The cited page numbers relate to it.

## Discovery of the Heads

The Heads were unearthed by Colin Robson and his brother Leslie in their garden one day in late May or early June 1971 (p. 14).[2] Colin was then about 11 and Leslie was about eight. Interviewed by Paul Screeton in 2012 (pp. 225-38), Colin recalled that each of the Heads was about the size of a cricket ball and of a similar, or slightly greater, weight.

While one of the Heads had a vaguely skull-like appearance, and a vaguely masculine-looking face, the other reportedly had a female, hag-like look (p. 14).

In his 2012 interview with Screeton, Colin said that that same day, he and his younger brother showed the items to Mrs Dodd, one of their neighbours at the adjoining house. Following her suggestion, they then took the Heads to Hexham Abbey, to see what the people there would make of them. As Colin recalled, the items remained at the abbey for a few days.

Hexham Abbey

## Events at the Dodds' home

Screeton (p. 32) explains that the Dodd household comprised Isaac and Nellie Dodd, then 43 and 42 respectively, and their six children, ranging in age from 15 to 7. It seems that the parents occupied one bedroom, and that the children occupied the remaining two (with three of them in each).

The eldest of Mr and Mrs Dodd's daughters was Sylvia. In March 2011, Screeton and some colleagues interviewed her and one of her brothers, Brian (pp. 30-5). By then, Sylvia's surname was Ritson. She was 15 at the time of the events in 1971. It seems that at night, the girls (except, perhaps, the youngest daughter, who slept in the room occupied by her brothers) would hear a 'pitter-patter', which their mother attributed to soot falling down the chimney. But soot didn't appear in the grate, which counts against that explanation. Sylvia also referred to a horrible feeling in the house and a sense that something was behind her. However, from what Screeton reports, it's not clear to me how long these experiences had been going on – whether they started *before*, or *after*, the Heads were found by Colin and Leslie Robson next door. (In June 2021, I wrote to Sylvia Ritson, seeking clarification about this, but I received no reply.) At any rate, leaving out a few other things, the main event concerned the mother, Nellie Dodd. On the night in question, she was sleeping with her youngest daughter, Marie, who was suffering from an ear infection. Nellie opened her eyes to see a strange creature – half-man and half-sheep – standing up on two legs. I shan't elaborate further, because the transcript of the interview doesn't give a very clear picture of precisely what happened. However, it appears that the encounter was brief and that the entity somehow exited the house via the front door.

## Events at the Robsons' home

As well as the parents (Albert and Jenny), the Robson household included two sons (the aforementioned Colin and Leslie) and an 18-year-old daughter, Judith. There was another son, Philip, but he may have left home by that point (p. 14). There was also a 23-year-old daughter, Wendy, but she was on her honeymoon when the Heads were found, and it's not entirely clear whether she (and her husband) resided at the house after their honeymoon (see below). I'll base this outline largely on what Colin Robson told Paul Screeton during the aforementioned 2012 interview.

Colin recalled that not long after he and Leslie had taken the Heads to Hexham Abbey, and before they got them back, members of the family were woken at night by screams from the Dodds' house. That was in connection with Nellie Dodd's encounter with the strange creature mentioned above. When the Heads were back with the Robsons, strange things started happening within their own home. A 'presence' was sensed. The Heads were placed in a display cabinet, but when family members came downstairs in the morning, they'd find them turned round, usually facing in the direction of where they'd been found. Locking the door of the room concerned (to prevent someone from upstairs coming down and mischievously tampering with the items) didn't stop the phenomenon from occurring.

Taps downstairs would turn themselves on during the night. On one occasion, there was a clatter from downstairs and Colin's mother went down to discover that a mirror, which usually hung to the left of the cooker, was lying, unbroken, on a frying pan on the cooker. If the mirror had simply fallen off the wall, it should have landed on a bench below, and broken. According to Colin, on another occasion, a picture fell on top of one of his sisters, with shattered glass covering a bed.

The most frightening thing that Colin recalled was an incident that occurred over a year, or maybe about two years, after the Heads were unearthed. About 10 people, including Colin, were in the living room when four or five items of bric-a-brac (little coloured bottles) jumped off the wall and struck the opposite one.

Colin also mentioned a couple of oddities concerning the garden. One of these was a sound (intermittent, I presume) coming from the back garden. It resembled that of a crying baby. According to Colin, it went on for years, although it hadn't been heard before the Heads were discovered (p. 231). Colin also referred, in vague terms, to reports of other people in the immediate neighbourhood 'seeing things in their house[s]', this only coming to light after the Heads were discovered, as he recalled (p. 237).

In 2011, Screeton managed to speak to Colin's sister Judith (pp. 25-6). Although she confirmed that anomalous phenomena had occurred, her recollections weren't fully concordant with Colin's. For example, she said that the Heads would be found facing each other, whereas Colin said they were usually found facing the spot where they'd been found. Judith recalled that her sister Wendy was then married and not living at the house. However, on p. 24 of his book, Screeton quotes from an account that Wendy sent to the forum of the magazine *Fortean Times*. In this, she said that in order to ensure that no one would tamper with the Heads during the night, she decided to put them under her bed, and that the next morning they were found to have moved from being under the top right of the bed to the bottom left – closer to where they'd been discovered. Of course, if true, this seems to suggest that Wendy was still living at the house, although I suppose that what she described may have occurred during a short visit.

I don't know how long the Heads remained at the Robsons' home, but they eventually wound up at the Museum of Antiquities at the University of Newcastle-upon-Tyne.

## Events at the home of Anne Ross

Dr Anne Ross (1925-2012) was an archaeologist and Gaelic-speaking Celtic scholar. She obtained her Ph.D. at the University of Edinburgh. She was the author of various books, and she held academic positions at universities. She spent her last years in Wales, sadly succumbing to dementia. She was married to the late Richard Feachem, an archaeologist, and she had two children, Charles and Berenice.

When she first heard about the Hexham Heads (in late 1971, it seems), Ross was a research fellow at the University of Southampton and was living with her husband and two children at 6 Rose Road in the Bevis Mount area of the city. It was usual for her to be asked to do research for museums, and that's apparently how she acquired temporary custody of the items (Screeton, *ibid.*, p. 38).

Although she didn't find anything unpleasant about their appearance, she took an immediate dislike to them. She left them in the box they'd arrived in, and put it in her study, intending to have the Heads 'geologically analysed' and then sent back north as soon as possible. A night or two after their arrival, she suddenly woke up, around 2 a.m., feeling very cold and very afraid. Looking towards the door, and aided by a light in the corridor beyond, she spotted a tall figure leaving the room. Her impression was that it was dark, like a shadow, and part animal, part man. She felt compelled to follow it and heard it going down the stairs. Then she saw it again, heading towards the kitchen. But she felt too afraid to go on. Instead, she returned to the bedroom and woke her husband. He searched the house, finding nothing, and there was no sign of any disturbance (p. 38). It's worth noting that at this point, Ross hadn't heard about Nellie Dodd's encounter with a strange entity.

The next incident occurred just a few days later. Ross's teenage daughter, Berenice, arrived home from school around 4 p.m. and saw a huge, dark, non-human entity on the stairs. It reportedly rushed down towards her and vaulted over the bannister. It landed with a soft thud, giving the impression that its feet were padded. It ran towards her room and she felt impelled to follow it. But at the door, it vanished. Ross and her husband arrived home around 6 p.m. After learning of their daughter's traumatic experience, they searched the house, but found no intruder (pp. 38-9). Phenomena continued. For example, Ross reported that her study door had burst open on several occasions, although there was nothing to account for it.

Anne Ross and her family lived at Rose Road for 20 years. At first, she found it to be a pleasant area, with families like her own. But the character of the neighbourhood changed, and the final straw came in 1986 when one of her cats (a kitten) was found with an 18-inch bamboo spear protruding from both sides of its body (pp. 46-7). A police inspector thought that it must have been fired from a crossbow. By then, Ross was no longer working at the university, and she and her husband put their house up for sale and moved to Wales. Of course, this distressing incident with the kitten may have had nothing to do with the Hexham Heads.

**Physical examination of the Heads**

In Chapter 6 of his book, Screeton discusses two reports about the physical make-up of the Heads. While the items were in Southampton, they were examined microscopically by Frank Hodson, Professor of Geology at the university there. His conclusions (in a report dated 10 March 1972) seemed consistent with Ross's view that the Heads were of ancient origin. But another report (dated 8 May 1974), by Dr Douglas Robson, Senior Lecturer in Geology at the University of Newcastle-upon-Tyne, deemed that the Heads had been made from 'an artificial cement'. Robson went further than Hodson in his examination, by removing some material from the Heads. Of course, Robson's findings gave credence to Des Craigie's claim that he'd made the items from building materials.

**Comments**

It may be that only some of the people who had contact with the Heads experienced strange phenomena. For example, there's no mention in Screeton's book (at least, not that I recall) of phenomena being reported from Hexham Abbey or the Museum of Antiquities in Newcastle when the Heads were there. Admittedly, though, it's possible that phenomena did occur in those places, but went unreported.

Interestingly, although it may be purely coincidental, one or more girls were present at each of the above-mentioned homes where manifestations occurred. Maybe a girl acted as a catalyst at each of those sites, as in some poltergeist cases elsewhere.

If the manifestations are to be attributed to a curse associated with the Heads, it was clearly of a Type 1 nature. But a Type 2 aspect can't be entirely ruled out. As noted, for example, Anne Ross eventually succumbed to dementia. However, that was decades later, and I doubt whether her illness was related to her temporary custody of the Hexham Heads in the early 1970s.

An intriguing question is why (for some people, at least) contact with, or possession of, the Heads resulted in their experiencing paranormal phenomena. If the Heads had, indeed, been ancient artefacts, it's possible to imagine a scenario in which some sort of curse was placed on them, maybe via an incantation such as: 'Let no one who disturbs these sacred items have peace until he or she restores them to their rightful place!' But, in itself, that wouldn't explain *how* the curse worked. As noted, though, it appears that the Heads may well have been made by Des Craigie.

Could it be that a tricksterish higher intelligence was behind the phenomena, and that it deliberately orchestrated things to give an impression that the Heads were carrying some sort of ancient curse? In other words, could it be that there was nothing intrinsically 'sacred' or special about the Heads, and they were simply stage-props for a manufactured drama?

## CASE 2: GHOSTLY PHENOMENA IN JARROW

In the previous chapter, I mentioned Darren Ritson and Mike Hallowell, who have investigated various poltergeist and haunt-type cases in their local area, the north-east of England. Their 'biggest case' was one involving poltergeist phenomena in South Shields, and was the focus of their book *The South Shields Poltergeist* (Hallowell & Ritson, 2009), the most recent edition of which is by Ritson (2020). In the aforementioned sequel, *Contagion* (Ritson & Hallowell, 2014), they refer back to the South Shields case, but they also discuss other cases that they've been involved with. One of these involved a family in Jarrow, which is near South Shields. Ritson and Hallowell refer to the couple concerned as Derek and Mandy, which are pseudonyms. The phenomena occurred at two successive homes. The case is of interest in its own right, but I'm mentioning it in this chapter because the phenomena may have been related to certain items (crime-related memorabilia) kept by Derek.

### Phenomena at a flat

It seems that the phenomena began early in 2007 when Derek and Mandy were living in a rented flat. At the time, Mandy was pregnant with her daughter, Ella (pseudonym). On occasions, Derek and Mandy sensed a presence in the flat, which made them feel uneasy. Entering the bathroom one evening in April 2007, Derek was surprised to find the window wide open. But neither he nor Mandy had opened it. In addition, a plastic panel that lined the side of the bath was detached and was now leaning against the bath. Several days later, Derek was entering the bathroom when he thought he heard his mobile phone ringing. By the time he retrieved it, it was no longer ringing and no missed calls were listed. At that point, he heard the sound of running water. Entering the kitchen, he saw water blasting into the basin from the cold water tap, although neither he nor Mandy had recently been in the kitchen.

In July of that year, after Ella was born, Derek awoke early one morning (around 3 a.m.) and saw a hooded male figure standing in the bedroom doorway, seemingly wearing a shroud of some sort. From what Derek could see of the face, it was yellow, with hollow eyes. It slowly disappeared. Looking back on the experience, Derek wasn't sure whether he was truly awake when he saw this figure or whether it was a dream. Interestingly, though, Mandy experienced a short episode of sleep paralysis that night, although she wasn't sure of precisely when: she woke up, finding herself unable to move, and then fell asleep again.

On 30 September 2007, the couple returned to their flat after visiting friends and sensed the 'presence' that they'd noticed before. Then, when they entered their bedroom, they were shocked to see various items on their bed, some of which they were adamant hadn't been on it when they left the flat. They included Ella's cot.

The next day, while speaking to a neighbour, Derek learned some things that he hadn't known before about the previous tenant of the flat. This had been a single man with a severe alcohol problem. His health was extremely poor and his behaviour had become erratic. He'd been in the habit of leaving the bathroom window open, even during bad weather, and he eventually got to the point of leaving the cold water tap running non-stop in the kitchen. Of course, there were parallels here with a couple of the odd events occurring during Derek and Mandy's tenancy (the bathroom window being found open, and the cold water tap in the kitchen being turned on). Hallowell wondered whether the former tenant developed jaundice as a result of alcohol-induced liver disease, and whether that accounts for the yellow appearance of the face of the figure seen by Derek early one morning in July.

## Phenomena in the couple's next home

The family moved to a terraced house not far from the aforementioned flat. More or less from the outset, they were troubled, intermittently, by a 'sense of presence'. It made Mandy feel afraid and vulnerable, whereas Derek would become depressed and moody. One evening, while the couple were sitting at their dining room table, the door of a recessed cupboard suddenly opened. Derek got up and shut it, but no sooner had he sat down than the door swung open again, but more forcefully than before. Derek ran a hand up and down an adjacent door, leading to the kitchen, but he felt no draught.

After several days, Derek started seeing something like a faint shimmer or movement in his peripheral vision. But when he turned his head, it would be gone. Mandy was also fleetingly seeing something in her peripheral vision. In her case, it resembled a shadow of a man, which would disappear before she could focus on it.

When the couple were downstairs, they sometimes heard what sounded like deep male voices, seemingly coming from upstairs, although they couldn't make out any words. At other times, they heard footsteps coming from the bedrooms upstairs. On several occasions, Derek dashed up the stairs and checked the bedrooms, but he never found anything amiss.

In addition to these recurrent manifestations, there were also one-off incidents. Perhaps the most dramatic involved a letter, and this is what highlights a possible 'cursed object' aspect to this case. Derek had an unusual hobby: collecting memorabilia associated with notorious criminals. It seems that he'd taken up this macabre interest more by accident than intention. To add items to his collection, he wrote to some convicted serial killers in the UK and the USA, thinking that if they responded, he'd have their autographs and entire letters to accompany them. A number of these murderers replied, and while some came across 'like really nice people', others were different. For instance, one of them was initially 'really pleasant', but then – in a subsequent letter, I presume – he said that he was going to arrange to have Derek killed! Naturally, Derek was scared and didn't write back.

One morning, a letter arrived for Derek. As he reached inside the envelope to extract it (at that point not knowing who'd sent it), the room suddenly felt icy-cold, and everything in it took on an icy, blue-white appearance. He felt that he was surrounded by something totally evil. Mandy and his mother were present, and they, too, reportedly experienced the same thing. It turned out that the letter was from one of Britain's most notorious serial killers. In suggesting that this letter acted like a 'cursed object', I'm not saying that the serial killer concerned (who isn't named in Ritson and Hallowell's book) consciously cursed Derek and his family. But maybe the letter carried with it, in some way, an evil or negative influence. This happened when Derek and Mandy were living in the second of the two homes, but I don't know whether it was the very first strange incident that they experienced there. As noted, though, they'd also experienced unusual phenomena at their previous home, and this particular letter presumably wasn't responsible for those manifestations. But maybe Derek's collection of crime-related memorabilia as a whole was exposing him and his family to malign influences. Indeed, Mike Hallowell suggested, as an experiment, that Derek should remove the memorabilia from their home, to see whether that would lead to fewer incidents or a cessation of the phenomena. However, it's not clear whether Derek ever acted on that suggestion. In an email to me in May 2021, Darren Ritson said that he and Hallowell doubted whether Derek would have disposed of his letters, since he loved them too much.

**Comments**

The evidence in this case doesn't hang entirely on the testimony of Derek and Mandy. Investigators also experienced manifestations at the terraced house occupied by the couple. I'll cite just two instances. On 25 March 2008, Darren Ritson and an associate of his called Mark Winter were standing just inside the door of the main bedroom when a pre-recorded videotape shot out from underneath Derek and Mandy's bed, landing at the investigators' feet. Ritson and Winter looked under the bed, but couldn't see anything to account for the phenomenon. And at one point, when everyone was downstairs, in the dining room, a loud thud was heard, seemingly coming from upstairs, followed by a gruff sound, suggestive of a male voice. Hallowell went upstairs to investigate, but encountered no one.

In an email to me (7 May 2021), Ritson explained that eventually things seemed to slow down and the couple became less worried about the phenomena. '[We said] we'd be at the end of the phone if they ever needed us […]. I guess it must have petered out as they never called us back. We eventually lost contact.'

This case highlights the difficulty that sometimes arises in distinguishing between place-linked hauntings and person-centred poltergeist disturbances. To some degree, the phenomena at both the flat and the terraced house had more of a 'haunt' flavour than a classic poltergeist character. However, unless we're to assume that, purely by chance, the family moved from one haunted residence to another, it appears that ghostly manifestations followed them from the flat to the terraced house. It would be interesting to know whether subsequent occupants of the flat also experienced ghostly phenomena there. If that were the case, we could be more certain that what Derek and Mandy experienced there was a place-linked haunting rather than purely person-centred phenomena. But maybe it was a bit of both – the flat may have been *potentially* haunted before Derek and Mandy moved in. Possibly one or other of them acted, unwittingly, as a catalyst, unleashing manifestations at the flat and enabling similar phenomena to occur at their next home as well. As noted, Derek's collection of crime-related memorabilia may have played a role in that.

## CASE 3: HAUNTED LOOMS

The following case is another of those cited by Darren Ritson and Mike Hallowell in their book *Contagion* (pp. 90-6). The following account is based on that source, and also on information from Mike Hallowell, conveyed to me by Darren Ritson.

The case was brought to Hallowell's attention in March 2008 by a contact of his called Steve Taylor. It concerned a craft shop ('Un Tesoro') in Blyth, Northumberland. The proprietor, Victoria Nesbitt (Vicky), informed Taylor that she'd bought two large looms from a university she'd attended and had set them up in a room above the shop. (A loom is an apparatus for weaving yarn or thread into fabric.) Before she acquired these items, there'd been no strange phenomena at the premises. After they arrived, a series of strange events ensued, leading Vicky to think that the looms (rather than the premises themselves) may have been 'haunted'. However, although I've used the plural form 'looms' rather than 'loom', it's worth bearing in mind that the phenomena may have been associated with only one of the looms. From the information available, it doesn't seem possible to know whether that was the case.

### Phenomena reported by Vicky

Strange noises, including voices, had been heard coming from upstairs. More than once, passers-by had reportedly seen an old woman looking down from the window of the room housing the looms. At one point, Vicky was in the room concerned, going about her work and listening to the radio, when something strange happened. A song was interrupted by what she described as 'an electronic hissing sound'. That was followed by a short period of silence, and then a female voice, which said just one word: 'Vicky'. Then, after a further burst of 'static', the music resumed.

Another incident concerned a scarf that Vicky had been weaving, using the older of the two looms. One morning, she sat down to resume the task and found a second scarf lying under the one she'd been weaving. She had no idea how it came to exist, and she couldn't see how it could have been woven without her one being removed, which it hadn't been.

## Investigation and aftermath

By arrangement, Steve Taylor, Mike Hallowell, and Hallowell's wife (Jackie) visited the premises on 28 March 2008.

There were two rooms at the top of the stairwell: on the left, an office and storeroom; and, on the right, the one that contained the looms, other bits of equipment, and a bench and kettle for making refreshments. The latter room had no door, just a blanket covering the entrance. The investigators noticed that this room felt much colder than the landing. Vicky explained that the room never got warm. However, prior to the arrival of the looms, the room didn't feel strangely cold. Taylor took readings with a digital thermometer, but they *didn't* show the room to be abnormally cold.

There were also some auditory phenomena. For example, recordings were made and some sounds were registered that weren't heard at the time (EVP); and at one point, a loud crack was heard after Taylor called on 'anyone present' to make a noise of some kind.

Taylor had the (psychic?) impression that someone called Edward had once lived in the building. Sometime later, Hallowell received an email from Vicky saying that she'd 'found' an Edward Spencer in a 1901 census. But she didn't specifically state that Spencer was listed as living at the premises in question.

As Hallowell was reading the email from Vicky, his wife came into the study and informed him that someone called Edward had tried to phone him while he was out visiting his mother. This was via their landline number. The caller declined to leave his number, saying that he'd ring back later, which he never did. Hallowell went to the phone and checked the log, which indicated that, for the last call received, the caller's number was withheld. That was strange, because the phone was set not to take calls from withheld numbers.

## Comments

Edward is a common name. It wouldn't, perhaps, be surprising if someone with that name had lived at the site at some point in the past. Therefore, if the census information confirmed that someone called Edward had lived there around 1901, it wouldn't be compelling evidence that Taylor got the impression of an Edward by psychic means. Also, of course, if the ghostly phenomena were wholly linked with one or other (or both) of the looms, the Edward in question may have had no bearing on the manifestations. However, it's intriguing that an Edward (or someone or something purporting to be an Edward) made the aforementioned mysterious phone call. This may have been an orchestration by a tricksterish intelligence that likes to 'play games' with people, including investigators; and that same intelligence may have been behind all of the phenomena.

## CASE 4: SANDWOOD BAY AND A NEARBY COTTAGE

In this section, I'll discuss some alleged incidents that occurred in, or were related to, the Sandwood Bay area in the far north-west of mainland Scotland. They share a common theme in that they involved ghostly phenomena being witnessed in connection with the acquisition, or attempted acquisition, of physical items. Arguably, the tales have more of a folklore ring than an air of authenticity. But I'll mention them for interest, and in case there's some historical truth in at least one or two of them. There are other stories about ghostly events in the Sandwood Bay area, but I shan't go into them here – because they don't relate to the notion of cursed or haunted objects (the principal focus of this chapter). But I've discussed the Sandwood Bay phenomena more generally, and in some detail, in a recent article in *Anomaly*, the journal of the Association for the Scientific Study of Anomalous Phenomena (McCue, 2021).

## The area

With extensive moorland, eye-catching mountains, lochs and rugged coastlines, Sutherland is a beautifully wild county in the northern Highlands of Scotland. Its remoteness and low population density have no doubt helped to protect it from the excessive development that's ravaging so much of Britain's countryside. Sandwood Bay is on the Atlantic coast of Sutherland, about six miles south-south-west of Cape Wrath, the north-western tip of the British mainland. It can be reached, on foot, from the hamlet of Blairmore, a few miles to the south-west. The route follows a track (with no vehicular access to the public) and then a path, which is well-maintained by the John Muir Trust. The bay is home to what's arguably Britain's most beautiful beach. An impressive sea stack, Am Buachaille ('the herdsman'), rises near the cliffs at the south-western end of the bay.

**Am Buachaille (zoomed) seen from Sandwood Bay**

In what follows, I'll mention not only Sandwood Bay but also what I've described as Sandwood Cottage, which is now a ruin. The 1:50,000 Ordnance Survey map of the area simply calls it 'Sandwood'. It's south of the bay and to the west of Loch Sandwood.

## Report 1 (Sandwood Bay)

Ronald Macdonald Robertson (1995, pp. 40-1)[3] refers to an occasion when a crofter and his son (unnamed) were gathering firewood from the beach. It was beginning to get dark and their pony suddenly became restless. Close beside them, the figure of a bearded man, dressed as a sailor, appeared from nowhere, loudly commanding them to leave his property alone. They reportedly dropped the wood and fled with the pony. This supposedly occurred in the summer, but Macdonald Robertson doesn't give the year. This alleged incident is also mentioned by Peter Underwood (1980, pp. 170-1; 1994, p. 212; 2013, p. 336). In his 1994 book, he dates it back to 'the late 1940s'. However, that may be conjecture, because, as I say, the report in Macdonald Robertson's book (which I presume was Underwood's source) doesn't give a date.

### Report 2 (unspecified location)

The late Andrew Green (1974, p. 247) refers to a story told by a shepherd, unnamed by Green. An Englishwoman had reportedly taken a piece of wood from an old wreck protruding from the sand at Sandwood Bay. After that, she regularly saw an old-fashioned sailor across the road from her home. The figure would pace up and down. Her conscience supposedly induced her to return the piece of wood, whereupon the sightings ceased. But Green doesn't name the witness, cite his source, or specify where the woman lived. And no dates are given.

### Report 3 (Edinburgh)

There are different versions of this report. Macdonald Robertson (1995, p. 43) refers to an Edinburgh woman, 'of high integrity and not given to exaggeration', who'd never visited Sandwood Cottage. She allegedly received a small piece of wood from its broken staircase. This had supposedly been posted to her as a souvenir from Scotland's most remote cottage.[4] But if she'd never been there, it could hardly have been a souvenir from her perspective! At the time of receiving it, she didn't know that the cottage was supposedly haunted, but strange phenomena then reportedly occurred in her home (which Macdonald Robertson describes as both a 'flat' and a 'house'): crockery fell on to the floor; knocks and heavy footsteps were heard at night; and, on one occasion, she allegedly sensed a strong smell of alcohol and tobacco smoke, and saw the dim outline of a bearded sailor, who shook the curtains violently before disappearing. However, despite these manifestations, she reportedly kept the piece of wood, which seems a little unlikely if she believed that its presence was causing such disturbances. Macdonald Robertson gives no dates for these alleged events and doesn't name the woman.

**Sandwood Cottage**

This story is also mentioned by Underwood (1980, p. 174). But instead of saying that the apparition shook the curtains, he states that it turned and faced the woman before disappearing. There are also a couple of additions: Underwood reports that the piece of wood 'now rattles and moves on occasions', and that the woman experienced phenomena in both her London flat and her house in Edinburgh. However, Macdonald Robertson's book makes no mention of her having a flat in London. It's likely, I think, that Underwood drew on Macdonald Robertson and was confused by (1) his use of both 'flat' and 'house' in respect of the woman's home, and (2) by Macdonald Robertson's reference to 'her city flat'. From the context, it's evident that this relates to Edinburgh, although Underwood may have wrongly assumed that it referred to London. But this doesn't explain the other additional feature in Underwood's version: the alleged rattling and movement of the piece of wood. Underwood briefly outlines the tale on p. 213 of his 1994 book. On p. 338 of his 2013 book, we can see a further mutation of the story: instead of being sent a piece of wood from Sandwood Cottage, the woman is now said to have taken it home after a visit!

Dane Love (2003, pp. 87-8) depicts the events somewhat differently. He identifies the property concerned as a tenement at 5 Rothesay Place (which is in Edinburgh's West End) and the people concerned as the Van Horne family. He states that, in 1958, strange things started happening soon after the arrival of some second-hand furniture they'd bought. The furniture had previously belonged to a sailor, who'd recently died. There were unexplained noises (usually tapping sounds). Then, ornaments that had been placed on the recently acquired furniture were found elsewhere. In the July of that year, the Van Hornes reportedly began to smell tobacco smoke. On enquiry, it was discovered that the aforementioned sailor was known as a pipe smoker. There were then visual manifestations: a bright ball of light was spotted and seemed to go from room to room; and in September, a tiny male figure was seen. It was only about a foot tall and was dressed in a brown jacket and red trousers. The family named it 'Gnomey'. It was reportedly seen on a number of occasions, and was witnessed by various family members. Love explains that by the beginning of the 1960s, the phenomena ceased almost as suddenly as they'd begun. There's no mention in this version of a piece of wood being received from, or having been taken from, Sandwood Cottage.

In his book *Edinburgh after Dark* (2010, pp. 40-1), Ron Halliday refers to two accounts concerning the Van Horne family at 5 Rothesay Place, one relating the phenomena to the purchase of second-hand furniture, and the other relating the manifestations to a piece of wood taken from a ruined cottage and sent to the family by a relative from the north of Scotland. Halliday speculates that the two versions may not be mutually exclusive: perhaps the purchase of furniture coincided with the arrival of the piece of wood. He states that the phenomena began in September 1958. However, according to Dane Love's version, the manifestations began earlier than that in 1958. Halliday's description of the alleged phenomena is fairly similar to Love's, but there are some elements not mentioned by Love. For example, on several occasions, drawers of a dressing table were allegedly seen to open and close by themselves. According to Halliday, Mrs Van Horne decided to burn the piece of wood sent from northern Scotland; and the next day, neighbours downstairs said that they'd been disturbed all night by knocking sounds from the area of her fireplace.[5] Unlike Love, Halliday doesn't mention sightings of a tiny male figure. I asked Ron Halliday about his source(s) for the story. He believes that he read it in a newspaper report.

CURSES, COINCIDENCES & MALIGN INFLUENCE

**Rothesay Place, Edinburgh**

## Comments

From an evidential point of view, these reports are rather unsatisfactory. Reports 1 and 2 are lacking in basic details, such as dates; and, as noted, there are different versions of Report 3.

## CASE 5: CURSED STONES IN SCOTLAND

Inverness is regarded as the capital of the Scottish Highlands. Its water supply comes from two lochs a few miles to the south-south-west: Loch Ashie and Loch Duntelchaig. In past years, there were reports of people having ghostly experiences in the vicinity of Loch Ashie. For example, there were stories about people witnessing a phantom battle near the north-eastern end of the loch. I investigated these reports, and I've discussed the alleged phenomena in some detail in Chapter 14 of my 2012 book *Zones of Strangeness*.

The *Highland News* newspaper (week ending 8 July 2006) carried the article reproduced below. It was written by Cameron Hay, then a journalist with the Highland News Group. It began on page 1 (with the heading 'Fears of evil ancient stones resurface as worried tourists send out SOS!') and continued on page 4 (with the heading 'Curse of the loch'). The interpolated comments in square brackets are my own.

The 'curse' of Loch Duntelchaig has rocked tourists again.

An English couple has posted a stone all they [*sic*] way back to Inverness, terror stricken that bad things may befall them for removing it from an ancient sacred area.

Local tourist industry staff have been asked to intervene to counter the curse legend by returning the memento for them.

It is the latest in a series of similar requests, adding to the eerie reputation of the beauty spot near Inverness.

There are a number of ancient burial grounds and cairns in the area and a local legend of sightings of phantom warriors.

The latest to be frightened by bad vibes are a couple from the Isle of Wight who picked up the rock as a souvenir from the edge of Loch Duntelchaig last year while on holiday.

Now they have posted it back to Inverness, with a request [that] it be returned to its rightful place.

An accompanying note to the city's tourist information centre read: 'Rock found near Loch Duntelchaig last year. Wife feels stressed when it is in the house. Maybe from the stone, so we have sent it back.'

And it is not the first time centre staff have dealt with this kind of request surrounding the Duntelchaig area.

Six years ago, a tourist from Belgium posted back a rock weighing 2lb after complaining it had cursed his family. The man revealed that since taking the stone his daughter had broken her leg, his wife had become seriously ill, and he had lost his job and broken his arm. [NB: It appears that the Belgian man *didn't* acquire the rock from the immediate vicinity of Loch Duntelchaig, but from a site some miles away – see below.]

After that story became public, the centre received other packages from concerned tourists asking staff to return stones.

A druid priest even offered to hold a ceremony to welcome back the rocks.

VisitScotland's customer advisor Bob Hunter-Doran told the *Highland News* this week: 'The man who sent the latest stone said that while he had picked it up from the water's edge, he reckoned it had rolled down from the site of an Iron Age or Pictish fort which once stood above the loch.

'It is possible he has done research on the area and thought the stone was cursed, so he decided to return it before it brought him and his wife any bad luck.

'Loch Duntelchaig is quite notorious for strange things going on and local legend has it that phantom warriors have been seen there. [NB: My research suggests that sightings of phantom warriors were associated with nearby Loch Ashie rather than Loch Duntelchaig.] It was once a well-populated area and has many burial mounds, chambered cairns and standing stones.'

But local author and city ghosts expert Davy 'The Ghost' Nish laughed at the suggestion that stones could be cursed and points the finger at fantasy writers.

He said: 'These things happen all around the world and you really have to take it with a pinch of salt.

'People believe what they want to believe and if they think something is cursed then bad things can happen.

'Thousands of stones are removed from Scotland every year and they can be regarded as lucky or unlucky.

'At least the stone is back where it belongs.'

The most dramatic story in this press report is that of the Belgian man and his family, who, coincidentally or not, experienced bad luck after acquiring a stone from the area. From the article, I presumed that the stone had been acquired from the shore of Loch Duntelchaig. However, in May 2021, I came across a BBC news item indicating that the stone was taken from the Clava Cairns, some miles away, to the east of Inverness.[6] I presume that the BBC article is referring to the main site, known as Balnuaran of Clava, which contains three large cairns (dating back about 4,000 years) and also some free-standing stones.

As indicated, the *Highland News* report mentioned a tourist information centre employee named Bob Hunter-Doran. The BBC article spells his surname with an added 's' ('Hunter-Dorans'). It quotes him as explaining that the Belgian tourist noticed a stone that, to him, looked like a Stone Age tool, which he took home as a souvenir. The family's run of bad luck apparently then began. Hunter-Doran(s) kindly acceded to the man's request to return the stone. Hunter-Doran(s) took the item home with him, but he left it in his garage overnight rather than risk taking it into the house. Then, the next day, he returned the stone to the Clava Cairns.

**The Clava Cairns**

## Comments

If curses can be activated by taking possession of stones, taking one from an ancient burial site such as the Clava Cairns might be riskier than removing a random stone from the shore of Loch Duntelchaig.

One might be tempted to laugh at the idea of people returning supposedly cursed stones to where they were obtained (via the assistance of one or more tourist information staff). However, such behaviour isn't completely irrational: if the person who uplifted the stone comes to suspect that it may be cursed, he or she might wish to play safe, by returning it.

## CASE 6: 'PELE'S CURSE', HAWAII

Hawaii, which is made up of 137 volcanic islands, is located in the Pacific Ocean. It became the fiftieth and most recent state of the USA in 1959. The largest of its constituent islands is itself called Hawaii. To avoid confusion, it's often referred to as 'Hawaii Island' or the 'Big Island'. Two of the world's most active volcanoes, Kilauea and Mauna Loa, are located on it, within Volcanoes National Park.

Although it's illegal to remove minerals from US national parks, visitors have sometimes taken away sand, bits of coral and other items from Volcanoes National Park. Some of them, at least, have come to regret it and have posted back, or have personally returned, the material they took. For example, according to an article in the *Wall Street Journal*, a California-based man called Steve Pariseau experienced a run of bad luck after taking away a black lava rock during a family holiday in Hawaii.[7] (The article isn't explicit about where the rock was acquired, but I presume it's referring to Volcanoes National Park.) Then, his sons began having behavioural problems, his marriage broke up, and his mother died. After hearing about 'Pele's Curse' – a belief that Pele, a mythological volcano goddess on the Big Island, would bring misfortune to people who plundered lava – he took the rock back, and his family fortunes immediately improved.

It seems that a belief in such a curse may not be confined to the removal of lava from the Big Island. It may apply to other natural materials as well, and it's perhaps considered to operate throughout the whole of Hawaii. A *HuffPost* article refers to a Karen Wade from the state of Washington, who returned from a family trip to the island of Maui in 2007 with a bottle of sand and a piece of coral.[8] Shortly after, her two dogs disappeared, she lost her home, and her marriage broke up. Subsequently (quite a few years later?), she returned to Hawaii with a new partner, and she left the sand at the beach that she'd originally taken it from. The holiday went well, and she was considering moving to Hawaii.

Jessica Ferracane, Hawaii Volcanoes National Park's public information officer, confirmed to the *HuffPost* that the park received returned rocks in the mail, as well as tiki figurines and other items. But she was dismissive of the notion of a curse, and she explained that there was no mention in any of the oral traditions that the goddess Pele would curse rocks.

## Comments

This case has clear parallels with Case 5. Although a fair number of people may have returned material (e.g. lava rocks) after experiencing bad luck, we don't know how many people took sand, lava rocks, and so forth *without* noticing any disturbing developments in their lives. It may be that the number of people who have taken materials and experienced no untoward effects vastly exceeds the number of those who think they were cursed.

## CASE 7: AN ILL-FATED SUBMARINE

The supposedly cursed object in this case wasn't a small item, but a German U-boat from the First World War. 'U-boat' is an English rendering of 'U-boot' (or 'Unterseeboot'), which literally means 'undersea boat'. I'm referring to a vessel known as *UB-65*, and my main source is Angus Konstam's readable 2005 book *Ghost Ships*. He relates the story of this ill-fated submarine on pp. 36-9. Whether all the details are historically correct, I don't know.

Construction of *UB-65* at the Vulcan Werft shipyard, Hamburg, began in late 1916 and she was launched in June 1917. As a coastal submarine, she was intended to contribute to the blockade of the UK. She was armed with ten 20-inch torpedoes and a 3.4-inch deck gun; and she had a 34-man crew.

While the vessel's keel was being laid, two dockyard workers were crushed to death in an accident. Later, three engineers died of asphyxiation when sulphuric acid fumes leaked into the enclosed space of the engine room. Soon after she set out from Bruges, Belgium, on her first patrol, a petty officer was washed overboard and drowned. During her first operational dive, the buoyancy tanks failed, and it took 12 hours to get her back to the surface. Furthermore, while she was submerged, her batteries leaked fumes again, with several crew members being temporarily overcome by them. Later, when she was in port, a torpedo exploded by accident, killing five crew members, including the second officer. After four months of repair work, she was ready to go to sea again. But then, there were reported sightings of the dead second officer's ghost. Back in port, the commanding officer was killed in an air raid. A crew member allegedly saw the aforementioned ghost in May 1918 and had to be sedated; and the following day, he supposedly jumped overboard and drowned. A few days later, another crew member was lost overboard.

On 10 July 1918, *UB-65* met her end off Cape Clear in what's now the Republic of Ireland. She was spotted on the surface by a submerged US Navy submarine. The latter set about moving into position to torpedo the German vessel, but before it could do so, *UB-65* exploded and sank.

According to Wikipedia, in the course of her operational career, *UB-65* sank six merchant ships, damaged six more, and also sank a Royal Navy vessel.[9]

## Comments

Although German U-boats inflicted heavy losses on Allied shipping in the two world wars, many of them were lost at sea. Therefore, in itself, the fact that *UB-65* and its crew met that fate isn't statistically remarkable, although there's uncertainty about how the fatal explosion occurred. Given the catalogue of prior accidents and deaths involving crew members and dockyard workers, one could say that the vessel was in some way cursed. Alternatively, of course, these mishaps could be regarded as nothing more than random bad luck.

The aforementioned Wikipedia article refers to two researchers, George Behe and Michael Goss, who have suggested that the stories about *UB-65* being haunted were fabricated by a journalist called Hector Charles Bywater.

## CASE 8: ÖTZI, THE ICEMAN

The case of 'Ötzi, the iceman' is one of those mentioned by J. W. Ocker in his 2020 book *Cursed Objects* (pp. 25-8). He hasn't got all the details right, and I've drawn on several sources in what follows.

On 19 September 1991, two German tourists, Erika and Helmut Simon, were walking at around 10,500ft in the Ötzal Alps, which extend from the South Tyrol region of northern Italy into Austria, when they came upon a human corpse that had been well preserved in the ice. Scientific examination showed that Ötzi, as he became known, was a staggering 5,300 years old. It seemed that he'd suffered a violent death, since there was an arrowhead embedded in his left shoulder, and there were various other wounds. It wasn't just his body that had been preserved by the ice – his clothes and other items (e.g. arrows, axe, and dagger) survived. He's estimated to have been 45 at the time of his death.

Initially, there was some dispute between the Italian and Austrian authorities over custody of the remains. But since the find occurred on the Italian side of the border, Ötzi eventually (1998) wound up at the South Tyrol Museum of Archaeology in Bolzano, Italy.

## Deaths following the discovery of Ötzi

Dr Rainer Henn, 64, a forensic pathologist who handled Ötzi's body, was killed in a car crash in 1992. He was reportedly on his way to give a talk about Ötzi.

Kurt Fritz, an Alpine guide, who organized the transport, by helicopter, of Ötzi's remains, was killed by an avalanche in the mountains in 1993. He was 52.

The aforementioned Helmut Simon died, aged 67, in the Austrian Alps in 2004 after getting caught in a blizzard and falling. Some sources (e.g. Ocker, 2020, p. 27) say that he was close to where he and his wife had found Ötzi in 1991. If so, that might be seen as giving credence to the notion of an 'Ötzi curse'. However, it appears that Simon's fatal accident occurred in a different part of the Alps, many miles from where Ötzi was discovered.[10]

Forty-five-year-old Dieter Warnecke, who led the team that searched for Simon, suffered a fatal heart attack within hours of the latter's funeral.

Archaeologist Dr Konrad Spindler (1939-2005) had been one of the first experts to study Ötzi. He died, in his sixty-sixth year, from complications related to a chronic illness (described as amyotrophic lateral sclerosis, or multiple sclerosis, depending on the source[11,12]).

Rainer Holz, a filmmaker who documented Ötzi's retrieval from the ice, died of a brain tumour when he was 47. I don't know the precise year of his death.

A California-born molecular biologist, Dr Tom Loy (1942-2005), was involved in the investigation of Ötzi. He identified four different types of blood on Ötzi's garments and tools, which accorded with his being killed in a skirmish rather than a hunting accident. Loy died at the age of 63 from complications related to a blood condition.

## Comments

At first sight, this catalogue of deaths might seem suspicious, and suggestive of a Type II curse being at work. However, some of the deaths occurred in or around 2005, some 13 or 14 years after Ötzi's remains were found. Two of the deaths involved mountain accidents. Mountain terrain is, of course, inherently dangerous, and in the case of Helmut Simon, the victim was caught in a blizzard at quite a high altitude. Regarding those who died of natural causes, their fatal ailments may have had nothing to do with their involvement in the discovery or examination of Ötzi. In the case of Tom Loy, the blood condition he suffered from has been described as lifelong and hereditary.[13] If that's the case, it doesn't, of course, make sense to attribute it to a curse related to his study of Ötzi.

The notion that Ötzi's remains have been the carrier of a curse would be stronger if there'd been a surprisingly large number of deaths among staff and visitors at the museum in Bolzano where the items are on display. But so far as I know, that's not the case.

## CASE 9: TUTANKHAMUN'S TOMB

I'm uncertain whether all the information I'll give about this case is historically correct, since sources seem to differ, or are unclear, about the precise details. Tutankhamun or Tutankhamen (colloquially known as 'King Tut') was an Egyptian pharaoh of the Eighteenth Dynasty. He reigned from about 1332 to 1323 BC. He was a child of about nine when he ascended to the throne. The cause of his death, some 10 years later, is unknown.

### The discovery of Tut's tomb

On 4 November 1922, a team headed by the British archaeologist Howard Carter discovered Tut's tomb. Carter was soon joined by his financial backer, George Herbert, the fifth earl of Carnarvon, and they cleared the way to the door. After days of digging, they entered an antechamber full of archaeological items, many of them made of gold. Another door, to the burial chamber, had one of its seals intact. On 26 November they entered it, finding it virtually undisturbed and its treasures untouched. On 17 February 1923, under the eyes of watching officials, Carter opened the door to the last inner chamber within the burial chamber, wherein lay a sarcophagus containing a coffin. Within it, there was a second coffin, which contained a third coffin, made of gold. King Tut's mummified body was found. But whether it was in the aforementioned sarcophagus and contained within the gold coffin, or in a different sarcophagus, I'm not sure. But regarding the matter of an alleged curse, this detail is essentially immaterial.

Despite rumours that anyone who disturbed the tomb would be cursed, its numerous treasures were catalogued and removed. They were displayed in a travelling exhibition whose permanent home is Cairo's Egyptian Museum.

## Deaths

Lord Carnarvon was bitten by a mosquito on or about 6 March 1923.[14] He subsequently nicked the bite site while shaving, which led to his death a few weeks later (on 5 April) at the age of 57. In a letter to the medical journal *The Lancet* in 2003, Ann M. Cox explained that, at the time, the earl's death was attributed to pneumonia related to a streptococcal infection, although pneumonia was thought to have been only one of the complications arising from the infection.[15] Cox noted that following a near-fatal car accident in 1903, Carnarvon was susceptible to frequent and severe lung infections. She also considered the possibility that he was exposed to aspergillus, a toxic mould, when he was in the tomb. However, she stated that there was no mention in Carter's diary of Carnarvon's illness until March 1923, and she thought that he would have become ill sooner if he'd been exposed to aspergillus in the tomb. In addition, she stated that of the 25 Westerners who first entered the tomb, Carnarvon was the only one to become ill or die soon after. Arguably, though, if his immune system was impaired, he would have been more vulnerable to aspergillus than the average person. Furthermore, he *wasn't* the only Westerner to die soon after visiting the tomb. The American railway magnate George Jay Gould died in France of pneumonia on 16 May 1923 after contracting a fever in Egypt, where he'd visited the tomb.

The Egyptian aristocrat Ali Kamel Fahmy Bey visited the tomb and was subsequently fatally shot by his French-born wife, Marguerite Alibert, in July 1923 at London's Savoy Hotel. But they reportedly had a tempestuous relationship, so the shooting may have had nothing to do with a curse.[16]

Ocker (2020, p. 37) notes that Carnarvon's half-brother, Aubrey, died in 1923 of what some said was blood poisoning, although Ocker doesn't say whether Aubrey himself visited the tomb. Archibald Douglas Reid, who X-rayed Tut's sarcophagus, died from a 'mysterious illness' in 1924; and the Governor-General of Sudan, Sir Lee Stack, who'd visited the tomb, was assassinated in Cairo, although Ocker doesn't give a date for that event. Ocker states that Georges Bénédite, a French Egyptologist, died after falling outside the tomb in 1926, and that Arthur Mace, who'd been a member of Carter's team, died in 1928 of what some said was arsenic poisoning.

In 1929, another half-brother of Carnarvon's, Mervyn, died of pneumonia, and a Captain Richard Bethell, who'd worked for both Carnarvon and Carter, died in what Ocker refers to as suspicious circumstances. Ocker adds that, months later, Bethell's father jumped out of a seventh-floor apartment, leaving a suicide note, saying that he couldn't stand any more horrors.

Without specifying details, Ocker (pp. 37-8) claims that the carnage didn't stop there, and that for anyone who visited the tomb, wrote about it, transferred items from it, or was related to someone involved, the word 'curse' appeared in his or her obituary. However, that appears to be rhetorical exaggeration. Indeed, Ocker goes on to say that Howard Carter lived on for almost another 20 years before dying of Hodgkin's disease (a type of blood cancer) in London. As the leader of the team that found the tomb, one might have expected him to be among the first to perish if there really had been a curse operating.

## Comments

Unlike the case of Ötzi, the iceman, where many of the supposedly suspicious deaths occurred years after the body was found, several of the deaths, in this case, occurred close in time to when the tomb was discovered and entered. However, as with other examples of presumed Type II curses, it's unclear whether a curse was actually at work.

James Deem (see note 12) cites some interesting figures provided by an Egyptologist called Herbert E. Winlock. If they're correct, they seem to count against the notion of a curse. According to Winlock, 26 people were present at the opening of the burial chamber (I presume this refers to the opening of the inner chamber containing Tut's sarcophagus), six of whom died within the next 10 years. Twenty-two of the 26 people were present when Tut's sarcophagus was opened, and only two of them died within the next 10 years. Ten of the 26 people present at the opening of the burial chamber watched the unwrapping of the mummy, and none of them died within the next 10 years.

## CASE 10: THE 'UNLUCKY MUMMY'

For this case, I'd advise readers to study David Castleton's detailed online article.[17] The case is also covered, in much less detail, by Ocker (2020, pp. 44-8). It features not a mummy as such, but a 'mummy board' – the lid of a coffin that had supposedly contained a mummified princess and priestess called Amen-Ra (after an ancient Egyptian sun god). She lived around 3,000 years ago, during Egypt's Twenty-first Dynasty. However, there's some dispute regarding her status – whether she was indeed a princess and priestess. And there's also some question as to whether her name really was Amen-Ra. At any rate, for many years, this item has been at the British Museum, where it's exhibit number 22542 and is named (slightly confusingly) as the 'Unlucky Mummy'. According to David Castleton, it's currently displayed in Room 62 of the museum. His article includes photographs of the artefact, which is about five feet long and depicts a fairly young woman with long hair and ornately patterned and brightly coloured clothing. It's not known what happened to her actual body.

**The legend**

Castleton explains that a lot of spurious or grossly exaggerated stories are associated with the 'Unlucky Mummy'. There's no one, clear-cut version of the tale. The following is a summary of parts of the legend. Castleton's article gives a fuller account.

At some point in the second half of the 19th century, an Oxford graduate called Thomas Douglas Murray (1841-1912) was on a trip to Egypt with two friends (or three friends, according to Ocker's book). They allegedly came upon the aforementioned coffin lid, which Murray bought. He arranged for it to be shipped to England. Murray injured an arm in a hunting accident while in Egypt. There was a delay in his getting medical attention, and gangrene set in, necessitating amputation of the arm.

Before they left Egypt, Murray and his friends supposedly heard disturbing rumours about the man who'd discovered the mummy. He'd allegedly died soon after touching its bandages, or had wandered off into the desert, never to be seen again. Murray's two friends supposedly died during the voyage back to the UK and were buried at sea.

However, as Castleton notes in his article, it's unclear to what extent, if any, Murray was really involved in the purchase of the 'Unlucky Mummy' and its being sent to England. But according to the legend, numerous people who came into contact with it in England died or experienced misfortune; and poltergeist-type phenomena supposedly occurred in its vicinity. But it seems that the story of the mummy board was conflated with another one, concerning an actual mummy, and that the alleged poltergeist phenomena were associated with the latter, not with the mummy board. (Whether there's any truth in this other tale, about an actual mummy, I don't know.) The 'Unlucky Mummy' wound up at the British Museum in 1889 or 1890, where it allegedly continued its career as a prolific serial killer and instigator of paranormal phenomena. But these claims were explicitly denied by Sir Ernest Wallis Budge (1857-1934), the museum's Keeper of Egyptian and Assyrian Antiquities. However, Castleton notes that Budge was fascinated by the supernatural, and was a member of the Ghost Club. Castleton quotes the late Peter Underwood (a prolific author of books on ghostly matters) as claiming that Budge 'certainly believed in Egyptian magic and the power of their dead'.

In good part, Castleton attributes the spurious and sensationalist stories about the 'Unlucky Mummy' to the aforementioned Thomas Murray and a friend of his, William Thomas Stead (1849-1912), a British newspaper editor whose writing style paved the way for modern tabloid journalism. Stead gave support to progressive social reforms, but it's said that he was prone to twisting facts, inventing stories, lying, and betraying confidences.[18] Like his friend Murray, he had a strong interest in spiritualism.

Stead was one of the victims in the tragic sinking of the *Titanic*, which struck an iceberg on her maiden voyage from Southampton to New York in April 1912. It was subsequently rumoured that the 'Unlucky Mummy' had been on board the ship. That notion, Castleton explains, seemed to come about from an article published in the *New York World* a few days after the ship went down. It contained an interview with a survivor, who recalled Stead talking about the 'Unlucky Mummy'. That appeared to give rise to a mistaken assumption that the item itself had been on board and was responsible for the disaster.

## Comments

When there's clear evidence that a story has been subject to distortion, fabrication, or exaggeration, it's tempting to dismiss it entirely. However, that risks throwing out the proverbial baby with the bath water. So far as the 'Unlucky Mummy' is concerned, it may be that there's no substance at all to the notion that it once did, or perhaps still does, exert a malign influence on people. But since there are uncertainties about its history, it would be unwise to be categorical.

Interestingly, though, a man called Noah Angell has collected reports of staff and visitors experiencing ghostly phenomena at the British Museum.[19,20] In some instances, these manifestations seem to have been linked with particular exhibits or parts of the museum, although I don't know whether any of the events have related specifically to the 'Unlucky Mummy'. The following are a couple of examples.

A security guard on patrol in the small hours found his attention directed to a wooden object, studded with iron nails, depicting a two-headed dog. It dated from late 19th century Congo and, according to curators, it symbolized mediation between the living and the dead. The employee felt some sort of power coming from it. He lifted his hand and directed it at the object, whereupon all the alarms in the gallery went off. Two days later, he and his brother visited the gallery during opening hours. He pointed at the item, and – once again – the alarms sounded.

A former member of staff, Phil Heary, told Angell of an occasion when he went up to the Egyptian mummy gallery in the middle of the night, to see whether things were all right. He found it 'absolutely freezing', although it was summer. It was so cold that he could see the breath coming out of his mouth, as if he'd walked into a freezer; and there was a smell he found indescribable. He rang security and explained that something was wrong. But by the time colleagues arrived, 'the presence' had vanished.

Angell was informed that the area housing Egyptian items seemed to attract people who wanted to divest themselves of objects they found creepy. He was informed that over 12 years, museum-quality items had been left by visitors on three occasions. At one point, someone had left behind the hand of a mummy, with an attached note explaining that he or she had found it among his or her grandfather's things after he'd died. It had reportedly brought misfortune (no details of this are mentioned) and the person wanted it to be properly disposed of.

## CASE 11: AN ALLEGEDLY CURSED CHAIR

A relatively well-known story from England concerns an oak chair that was supposedly cursed by an 18th-century murderer, Thomas Busby. Ocker (2020, pp. 123-6) discusses the case, and accounts of it can also be found on the internet – for example, in a *Northern Echo* article by Stuart Minting.[21] Unfortunately, this is another of those curse tales that has different versions and where it's difficult to distinguish clearly between folklore and historical fact.

Since 1978, the chair has been on display at the Thirsk Museum in North Yorkshire, where it is safely suspended part way up a wall, meaning that visitors can't deliberately or accidentally sit in it and risk succumbing to the supposedly fatal curse associated with it. According to Minting's article, it had recently attracted an unsuccessful $1m offer from an American collector, and it had drawn the attention of a film crew from Japan.

Before going to the museum, the chair was to be found at the Busby Stoop Inn, three miles west of Thirsk. The pub gets its name from Thomas Busby, who was publicly hanged in 1702 for the murder of an associate, Daniel Auty. The men were involved in counterfeiting coins at nearby Kirby Wiske. It has been claimed that Busby was married to Auty's daughter, and that Auty and Busby fell out over the latter's ill-treatment of her. However, Minting's article notes that the museum's curator, Cooper Harding, is unaware of any evidence confirming that Auty was Busby's father-in-law. The murder may have arisen simply from a dispute over the spoils of their criminal activity.

It's said that when Busby was on his way to be hanged, he was granted a last request, a glass of ale at the inn that came to be named after him. After sitting in his regular seat and downing his drink, he uttered a curse: that sudden death should come to anyone who dared to sit in his chair. After the hanging, Busby's body was dipped in tar (to slow down its decomposition), placed in an iron frame, and hung from a 'stoop' (pole).

The chair in question supposedly remained at the pub for centuries, acquiring a bad reputation. For example, Minting notes that two RAF pilots who sat in it in 1967 were killed after driving away, their vehicle having crashed into a tree. A few years later, a builder reportedly accepted the challenge of sitting in it, and fell to his death from a roof within hours of doing so. A cleaner is said to have stumbled into it while mopping, and subsequently died of a brain tumour.

The long-serving landlord, Tony Earnshaw, consigned the chair to the cellar in the 1970s. But a beer delivery man reportedly sat in it there and was allegedly killed, just minutes later, in a crash a few miles away.

## Comments

Minting learned from the museum's curator, Cooper Harding, that assizes records for 1702 had been lost, so details of when and where Busby was hanged are unclear. Furthermore, no contemporary documentary evidence of his uttering a curse has come to light. Minting's article explains that Dr Adam Bowett, a furniture historian, examined the chair and concluded that it was made after 1840, many years after Busby's death.

Even if several people did die very soon after sitting in a particular chair at the pub, that wouldn't, in itself, mean that the chair was cursed. After all, it may be that over the centuries, many more people sat in it, *without* dying prematurely. Occasional instances in which people died soon after sitting in the chair may have been remembered and spoken about, but occasions when that didn't happen may have soon been forgotten. Furthermore, if the pub attracted passing trade and some of those customers sat in the chair, it's unlikely that information would be available about what subsequently happened each and every one of them.

## CASE 12: THE DYBBUK BOX

This case, for which I've drawn on several sources, concerns what Ocker (2020, pp. 103-8) describes as 'a portable wine cabinet', about the size of a backpack. It's been referred to as a 'dybbuk box' (or 'dibbuk box'). A 'dybbuk', in Jewish folklore, is an evil spirit.

This story allegedly goes back to the years of World War II, but I'll start with a man called Kevin Mannis in the early 2000s. He was then the owner of an antique furniture finishing store. He's also been described as a professional writer, actor, and recording artist. He claimed that in 2001 he'd attended an estate sale in Portland, Oregon, following the death of a 103-year-old Polish-born woman who'd owned the house concerned. Mannis spoke to a granddaughter of hers, who explained that, along with others, the woman had escaped from a Nazi concentration camp during World War II and had somehow got to Spain, whereas the rest of her family (parents, siblings, husband, two sons, and a daughter) had been killed.[22] She remained in Spain until the end of the war, and it was there that she purchased the 'dybbuk box'. She told her granddaughter that she should never open it.

Mannis bought the item. The box had two doors and a small drawer at the bottom, and it was made in such a way that if one of the doors was opened, the other one and the drawer did so as well. The doors had carvings representing clusters of grapes, and at the back of the box, there was an engraved Jewish prayer. The box contained various items, such as locks of hair and a small granite statue engraved with the word *shalom* (meaning 'peace'), although this appeared in Hebrew letters, not in English.

For Mannis, if we're to believe his story, his acquisition of the box didn't bring peace.[23] For example, his shop was damaged in what sounds like a shortlived burst of intense poltergeist-type activity, and he began to see shadowy forms, smell ammonia, and have nightmares featuring a hag. He tried to give the box away or sell it, but the people concerned returned it to him. One of them was his mother, who suffered a stroke after being given the box as a gift.

Mannis posted the box for sale on eBay in 2003. In describing it, he went into considerable detail regarding his experiences and concerns about it (see note 23), and he expressed the hope that someone more knowledgeable about the paranormal would relieve him of it. It was bought, for $140, by a Iosif Nietzke, said to have been a Missouri college student. Less than a year later, Nietzke sold it for $280, also via eBay. During his ownership of the item, he and his roommates allegedly experienced various problems, such as allergy-like symptoms, lengthy spells of torpor, and electronic devices frequently 'dying'. The difficulties reportedly escalated to hair loss and visions involving dark, blurry things.

It was Jason Haxton, the director of a museum of osteopathic medicine at a Missouri university, who bought the box from Nietzke. He gave it considerable publicity by writing a book about it (Haxton, 2011), creating a website devoted to it,[24] and discussing it in interviews. Although he attributed some personal physical ills to the box, he also reported a beneficial effect: he asserted that, for him, it had reversed the ageing process! The story of the box was fictionalized in a 2012 horror film, *The Possession*. From searching on the internet, I discovered that a short (1 hr) film called *Dybbuk Box: True Story of Chris Chambers* was released in 2019.[25] I haven't seen it myself, and I don't know whether there's any truth in what it portrays. But I imagine that, to some degree, the screenplay was inspired by the case under consideration.

Zak Bagans, star of the American reality TV show *Ghost Adventures*, bought the box in 2017 for his 'Haunted Museum' in Las Vegas. When Ocker visited the museum, the tour guide said that the doors of the box had come ajar of their own accord. In 2018, the rapper Post Malone encountered the box while guest-starring in an episode of *Ghost Adventures*. He seemed disturbed by it, and he subsequently experienced some mishaps, such as an emergency landing in a plane and a car accident.

## Comments

If a curse played a role in the events and experiences outlined above, it may have been associated with one or more of the items contained within the box rather than the box itself. (I'm assuming that when the box changed hands, the new owners also received its contents.)

For sceptical views on this case, I'd refer readers to articles by Brian Dunning[26] and Kenny Biddle.[27] Dunning notes that the very notion of a box being inhabited by a dybbuk is nonsensical, given that a dybbuk is supposed to be a disembodied spirit that possesses someone else's body, not an inanimate object.

There's a degree of mystery associated with the above-mentioned and unusually named Iosif Nietzke. When he re-listed the box on eBay, he said that he'd blogged about his experiences with it. But Dunning wasn't able to find any such blog. A freelance entertainment writer, Leslie Gornstein, wrote a short article about the case for the *Los Angeles Times* in 2004. According to Dunning, she tried, repeatedly, to contact Nietzke, without success. Dunning adds that apart from references to the dybbuk box canon, the Internet has basically no record of Nietzke.

Kenny Biddle (note 27) contends that the dybbuk box isn't a Jewish wine cabinet, but a mini-bar dating back to the 1950s or 60s. He suggests that Kevin Mannis's story was invented to boost the item's selling price on eBay, and that its reputation was 'propelled into paranormal pop culture' by Jason Haxton's book and then by the aforementioned film, *The Possession*.

Even if we assume that people such as Mannis and Haxton have reported in good faith, it's hard to know whether, or to what extent, any sort of curse was at work. Take, for instance, the stroke that Mannis's mother allegedly suffered after being given the box as a gift. That could have been purely coincidental. If people believe that an item in their possession is cursed, they might be inclined to blame it for mishaps that have nothing to do with it, and the power of suggestion could lead to their feeling out of sorts in its presence.

## CASE 13: A CURSED BONE

A relatively well-known 'curse' story concerns events that allegedly began in 1936 when Sir Alexander Hay Seton (1904-63) and his first wife, Zeyla (1904-62), were visiting a tomb in Egypt. During the visit, and unbeknown to Seton at that point, his wife took away a piece of bone from the remains of a skeleton. In outlining the story here, I've drawn on an Internet article by someone calling himself 'Ian'.[28] He quotes from a document or publication written by Seton himself. For more information, I'd refer readers to the online source. The following distillation is based on Seton's account.

Zeyla showed her husband the piece of bone she'd removed from the tomb. To him, it looked like a digestive biscuit, although it was slightly convex and shaped like a heart. Some weeks later, after they'd finished their holiday in Egypt, the Setons had some friends round for supper at their home in Learmonth Gardens, Edinburgh. Zeyla showed them the item. Just as the friends were leaving, a large piece of the roof parapet crashed down, landing about two feet away from those present.

The next incident occurred a few nights later. The Setons had gone to bed, but a person referred to as 'Nanny' rushed upstairs to say that she'd heard someone moving about in the drawing-room. Seton went downstairs to check, but found nothing. He remembered that later that night, he heard a crash, but thought nothing of it at the time. But the following morning, a table was found on its side, with the small glass case that had contained the bone beside it. The piece of bone was also on the floor.

**Learmonth Gardens, Edinburgh**

A few weeks later, and occurring over some nights, there were unexplained noises. Shortly after, Seton's nephew, Alasdair Black, visited for a few days. One morning, he announced that he'd seen a strangely dressed person going upstairs the night before.

Not long after that, it seems, there was a night when items were found disturbed in the drawing-room: chairs had been upset, books had been flung about, and in the middle of the chaos was the bone. After some weeks with no activity, noises were again heard coming from the drawing-room. Zeyla had the idea of moving the items that had been flung about, except the heavy chairs, to her husband's sitting room on a lower floor. That was done, and the bone was included among the things moved. However, after a week or so, Seton got fed up with having his sitting room so cluttered, and said that he'd move the items back the next day. However, that night, furniture was disturbed in his sitting room. As usual, the bone was found on the floor. Seton told his wife that he was going to burn it, but that drew a storm of abuse from her, so he left for his club and some drinks.

When he arrived home, he discovered that there'd been further activity: one of the legs of the table on which the bone lay had been cracked. After a few weeks without further activity, there was another incident in the drawing-room. Among other things, the bone had been broken into about five pieces.

According to Seton, he gave 'the Bone' (I presume he meant the fragments of the bone) to a reporter from the *Scottish Daily Mail*. But it was returned to him, apparently because the reporter had become seriously unwell.

On the evening of Boxing Day, the Setons had people round for dinner, with cocktails being served in the drawing-room. To Seton's disgust and dismay, his wife had got a friend of hers to mend the bone, as far as possible. She'd placed it on a table opposite the door leading into the drawing-room, which provoked conversion about it. There came a point when the table and bone slammed into a wall, although no one actually saw it happen.

Although not a Catholic himself, Seton suggested that his uncle, Father Benedict of Fort Augustus Abbey, come and 'exorcise' whatever was behind the activity. Permission for that was granted, and a ritual was performed (although I don't know whether it was a formal exorcism). The bone was blessed and then incinerated by Seton. There were no more poltergeist-type disturbances. However, Seton noted that from 1936 onwards trouble always seemed to be around the corner.

## Comments

Clearly, if this report can be believed, we could class the poltergeist-type effects as manifestations of a Type I curse. It's hard to know for certain, but there may also have been a Type II aspect to the curse, particularly if it's true that a newspaper reporter became seriously ill after being given the bits of bone.

# CHAPTER 6

# CURSED BY BLACK-EYED CHILDREN

There are stories about people encountering children or child-like entities with totally black eyes or with black cavities where the eyes should be. They've been dubbed 'black-eyed children' or 'black-eyed kids' (BEKs). The American researcher David Weatherly has brought together an interesting collection of witness reports in his book *The Black Eyed Children*, the second edition of which was published in 2017. Judging from some of the accounts that he cites, it appears that BEK encounters can presage, or bring about, bad luck. However, that may not be typical.

## HISTORICAL ASPECTS

Stuart Ferrol (2014) claims that the first reported BEK sighting came from the journalist Brian Bethel in his hometown of Abilene, Texas. Bethel's experience, which reportedly occurred around 1996, is outlined below. Taking a sceptical view, Jenny Coleman (2014) links BEK reports with aspects of popular culture in that decade and subsequent years. For example, she notes that black-eyed characters featured in the fictional TV series *The X-Files* and *Buffy the Vampire Slayer*, and in the 2004 film *The Grudge*. She contends that it's conceivable 'that the 1990s, with the birth of the Internet and these kinds of cultural influences, [...] brought forth the mythos of the Black-Eyed Kids'; and she suggests that they 'have all the hallmarks of [an] urban legend'.[1] This presumably means that she doubts whether there've been any genuinely paranormal BEK incidents. But if there's a tricksterish intelligence behind many anomalous phenomena, it may draw on contemporary folklore themes, using them as templates for its theatrical paranormal displays. In any event, in his book *Strange Intruders*, Weatherly (2016, p. 119) claims that he's found BEK accounts predating both television and the Internet. One of the cases that he discusses in *The Black Eyed Children* (pp. 43-7) dates back to around 1950. The witness was dead by the time the case came to Weatherly's attention, but the story had been passed down over the years, and Weatherly was able to speak to several of the man's relatives.

## CHARACTERISTICS OF BEK ENCOUNTERS

Judging from Weatherly's book, a typical BEK encounter might proceed as follows: You're at home, alone, around sunset, when you hear a steady knocking on your front door. You wonder why the caller hasn't rung the bell. When you open the door, you see two children, about 12-14 years old. One of them acts as their spokesman. He asks you to let them in, perhaps to watch some television or use the phone. You're familiar with the local children, but you've never seen this pair before, and something seems wrong. The spokesman repeats his request, but he doesn't respond to questions from you seeking more information. Initially, he was polite, but his tone becomes importunate (e.g. 'Look, just invite us in – this won't take long!'). He and his companion look up, and you notice that their eyes are completely black. Shocked, you close the door on them and lock it. For a while, you hear further knocking on the door. Badly shaken, you fear that you may encounter these sinister-looking children again. But for most witnesses, the encounter will be a one-off event.

It's not just people's homes that BEKs seek to enter. For example, as in the incident reported by Brian Bethel (Case 1, below), they may tap on the window of a parked car and ask the driver to invite them in for a ride. In some cases, witnesses notice a foul and quite persistent smell at the spot where the entities were seen. Judging from reports in Weatherly's book, this odour is noticed *after* the BEKs have disappeared, not during the encounter itself.

Again, judging from Weatherly's case collection, it appears that BEKs can move from one spot to another, or disappear, within a very short space of time. For example, someone might be speaking to BEKs and then fleetingly look away; when the witness returns his or her gaze to the entities, they might be much closer than they were before. Another oddity is that they may seem to multiply in an instant: after seeing two BEKS, a witness might avert his or her gaze fleetingly, and then see three of them.

Paranormal entities, such as 'alien greys' and apparitions, can reportedly show up, uninvited, within people's homes. There are also accounts of drivers seeing apparitions within their vehicles (McCue, 2018, pp. 74-9). However, Weatherly (2017, p. 149) claims that BEKs need to receive an invitation to 'come in' before doing so. But maybe there's more than one type of BEK, and perhaps this requirement doesn't apply to all of them, as in Case 2, below (if it can be believed).

It's worth noting that there have also been reported sightings of black-eyed adults (see Case 4).

## Case 1: Brian Bethel's experience

Brian Bethel can be heard discussing his experience in an interview with Ryan Sprague in episode 29 of an Internet show called *Somewhere in the* Skies.[2] The incident allegedly occurred in or around 1996, probably in the spring or summer, between 9.30 and 10 p.m. Bethel had parked his car near what he describes as a 'theatre marquee', where films were shown. He was writing out a cheque, which he intended to pop into a drop slot to pay an Internet bill. There was knocking on the driver's side window of his car. He looked up to see two boys, probably about 9-12 years old. They were wearing hooded tops and jeans. Bethel lowered his window somewhat. One of the boys, acting as their spokesman, said that they wanted to see a film but had forgotten their money, and could Bethel drive them to their mother's house, so they could collect their money and return to see the film? For some reason, Bethel felt very apprehensive. Eventually, the boy acting as their spokesman became more insistent, saying, 'Now, look, mister, we're just two little kids. We don't have a gun or anything.' With his fear mounting, Bethel asked what movie they wanted to see. It was *Mortal Kombat*. However, the boys' request didn't make sense, since by then it was about 9.50 p.m. and the last showing of the film would have already begun. Furthermore, if Bethel had driven the boys to their home and then back, they would have missed even more of the film. It was at this point that Bethel noticed that they had reflective black eyes. Gazing at them was like looking into a void. He felt panicky. He muttered one or two excuses and rolled up the window. The boy acting as the spokesman then slammed on it repeatedly. Bethel heard him say that they couldn't enter unless he told them that it was all right to do so. Bethel quickly reversed out of his parking spot and drove away. Glancing in his rear-view mirror, he saw no sign of the BEKs.

Bethel wrote up an account of his experience and posted it to an email group (in 1997, it seems, judging by what he told Ryan Sprague). But his story soon received much wider attention on the Internet.

Weatherly (2017, pp. 223-4) quotes Bethel regarding the aftermath of his encounter. Like other witnesses, he reported features of post-traumatic stress (e.g. insomnia and flashbacks). He also mentioned possible paranormal after-effects, such as equipment tending to malfunction or behave strangely when he was being interviewed about the incident. In addition, he referred to a run of bad luck, although it's not clear to me whether he meant bad luck following the BEK encounter itself, or bad luck ensuing when he went public about his experience. He explained that at the time of the encounter, he was going through considerable spiritual and mental changes. In his view, they were, in part, what attracted the BEKs to him. He was grateful for the experience, because it had taught him to trust his intuition.

## Case 2: A girl in the woods

**Cannock Chase, Staffordshire**

In his booklet *The Black Eyed Child of Cannock Chase*, Lee Brickley (2021, pp. 43-6) includes an anonymous report from a driver, of unspecified gender, who allegedly saw what appeared to be a small child-like figure, wearing an old-fashioned dress, in some woods beside Stafford Road, Cannock, around 2 a.m. on 14 February 2020.[3] It was snowing at the time. Thinking the child might be lost or in distress, the driver pulled over and got out of the car. But there was no sign of the girl. The witness walked up and down the road for a few minutes, gazing into the woods, but couldn't see the girl. He or she also called out, but got no response. This person then resumed his or her journey. Eventually, there was a giggle from the back seat. In the car's rear-view mirror, the driver reportedly saw the girl that he or she had spotted previously. She had a white face and black eyes.

There's nothing in the account to suggest that the figure had sought permission to enter the car. At any rate, the driver allegedly stopped, unbuckled his or her seatbelt, and turned round. However, the black-eyed girl was gone. The driver got out and opened the back seat doors, but there was no sign of anyone. The driver looked around, but still couldn't see the girl.

I'm not sure that this tale can be believed.[4] But if it is true, it means that not all BEKs require permission to enter a vehicle, which raises the disturbing possibility that they can also turn up, uninvited, *within* people's homes. However, leaving aside the matter of the black eyes, the story sounds more like a ghostly experience than an encounter with BEKs of the type described by David Weatherly. That's also the case in the following report.

## Case 3: A ghostly boy in a forest

This alleged sighting features in 'Satanic Swamp', an episode of a TV series called *Hometown Horror*. First screened in 2019, the episode deals with Freetown State Forest in south-eastern Massachusetts. The forest has a reputation for strange and sinister activity. The incident in question occurred on a sunny day in 1984. Freetown resident John Brightman was cycling with two friends in the forest. He got ahead of his companions and stopped to wait for them. He heard a sound like a branch breaking and then saw a male, child-like figure. It was perhaps three and a half or four feet tall. He could see through it. The eyes were piercing black. He looked away momentarily, but the figure was gone when he looked back.

## Case 4: Black-eyed adults

In his book *Strange Intruders*, Weatherly (2016, pp. 101-4) cites the case of a witness called Marcel, who reportedly had an uncanny experience in the late autumn of 2010 while renting an apartment in New York City. Across the hall, he had a somewhat strange male neighbour, who was eventually joined by a woman of Asian appearance. One day, the woman dropped a grocery bag in the hall. Some cans of meat and fish fell out of it. Marcel bent down to pick some of them up for her. The man angrily told him to leave it to the woman. Marcel looked up, noticing that the man's eyes were completely black. Then, he noticed that the woman's eyes were also black, although they reverted to normal within seconds. The odd neighbours moved away, but Marcel developed claustrophobia and an aversion to meat.

## BAD LUCK FOLLOWING BEK ENCOUNTERS

Weatherly cites cases in which people experienced bad luck very soon after BEK encounters. Assuming that the cases have been accurately reported, they raise interesting questions: Was the bad luck merely coincidental? Was the BEK encounter an omen of imminent misfortune? Or did the BEK(s) somehow bring about the bad luck?

### Case 5: A BEK who *was* 'invited in'

Weatherly (2017, pp. 142-50) doesn't give a date for this case, although he indicates that his informant, Sharon, an Iowa-based nurse, contacted him about a year and a half after the events in question, which began on a Sunday afternoon.

With her young son in her car, Sharon called at a convenience store for some milk and cereal. She left her son in the vehicle and popped into the shop. When she returned, she started the engine and simultaneously looked in the rear-view mirror. She was stunned to see a young boy with black eyes staring at her coldly from the back seat. He was sitting unusually close to her son. Trying to control her panic, she jumped out of the car, jerked open the back door, and quickly yanked her son out. Pulling him with her, she rushed back to the store, where she told the sales assistant that someone was in her car. After ascertaining from Sharon that the intruder wasn't armed, he went out and checked the vehicle. No one was in it, and the rest of the parking area was empty. The assistant reached into the car, switched off the engine, removed the keys, and closed the open doors. He cautiously looked around the sides and the back of the building, seeing no one. He was minded to phone the police, but Sharon managed to dissuade him. Although she didn't mention this to the sales assistant, she feared that the police would think she was lying or deluded and that word about it would get out.

Although she wanted to get her son home, Sharon couldn't bring herself to do so in the car involved in her fright. She rang her husband, Tom, who quickly arrived on the scene. Following a bit of conversation with him, she set off with their son in Tom's truck.

After speaking to the sales assistant and then looking around the parking area, Tom got into Sharon's car and started the engine. He then noticed a smell, like soiled nappies, which came at him in waves, and which seemed to get progressively worse. He looked around the car again, but found nothing to account for the odour. He rolled down the windows and set off for home. But after a few miles, he was involved in an accident, with his car being 'totalled'. A passing driver spotted the wreckage and rang for help. Tom was taken to a hospital. He'd struck his head during the accident, and he had a headache, but it cleared up later that evening. He couldn't remember the accident itself. He was kept in hospital overnight for observation.

Sharon learned from her son that the BEK wanted a ride to their house. The son thought that they could play, and invited the stranger into the car. He didn't recall noticing anything special about the child's eyes. This raises the question of whether BEKs (or the intelligence behind them) can transform their appearance or manipulate the way people perceive them.

In the days that followed Tom's release from the hospital, his son became unwell, experiencing things such as high fevers, stomach aches, and sores on his body. However, it seems that medical personnel were unable to make a definite diagnosis. But Tom and Sharon related his problems to his contact with the BEK. They started praying for him regularly, and they asked other family members to pray for him as well. After some weeks, he recovered.

## Case 6: A flat tyre and a fire following a BEK encounter

This case (Weatherly, 2017, pp. 110-2) is also undated. The witness, Hector, was originally from Mexico. He was working at his family's Mexican restaurant in San Antonio, Texas, when he had his encounter. He was told by one of the cooks that a boy was hanging around behind the premises. Hector went out to look, but he saw no sign of the boy. He went back into the restaurant. Just as he closed the door behind him, he heard a loud knock on it, which was strange, since he didn't know how someone could have reached it so quickly, given that there was nothing close to the building that someone could have hidden behind.

Hector opened the door to see a boy in a hooded sweatshirt. The boy looked at Hector and seemed to push his face forward. He had solid black eyes. Speaking in Spanish, he said that he knew that Hector would be the one to open the door and that now he was 'in for it'. The boy started laughing loudly, which scared Hector, who then slammed the door shut.

After Hector left work that evening, his vehicle had a flat tyre, although his tyres were new, having been fitted only two weeks previously. Furthermore, he didn't recall running over anything that might have damaged the tyre. At his home that night, the oven in the kitchen caught fire mysteriously. Fortunately, the fire was extinguished before it did further damage. (Hector seems to have been referring to the family home.) They – Hector and other family members, I presume – went to a church for midnight mass. He said numerous prayers and lit a candle to make the harm go away.

Hector's brief encounter with the BEK made him take a more spiritual path in his life. Weatherly quotes him as saying that he believed that a higher force had sent the BEK to wake him up and send his life in a different direction. That's an interesting idea, and it's reminiscent of Brian Bethel's comment about his own experience (see above). But from a theological perspective, it might be questioned: would a good, higher power use something destructive to draw someone to a better path?

**Case 7: Touched by a BEK**

Without giving a date, Weatherly (2017, pp. 150-3) cites the case of a woman called Beth. Two BEKs, one male and one female, showed up at her door and insisted on entering. But Beth refused. One of them, the girl, grabbed Beth's wrist. Although the grip wasn't hard, the BEK's hand was ice-cold. Beth broke free and retreated into her apartment. She was unable to sleep that night. The next day, she became ill with a stomach virus. The following day, her car was broken into and her laptop was stolen from it. And the day after that, she lost her job and her boyfriend left her (after a seven-year relationship).

Less than a week after she lost her boyfriend, Beth had a session with a female psychic. Beth hadn't mentioned the BEKs, but about 12 minutes into the session, the psychic, looking scared, declared that Beth had run into two kids with black eyes. The psychic believed that they'd cursed Beth, and she said that there was nothing she could do for her. However, she suggested that Beth see someone else, such as a priest. She mentioned a few people Beth could contact. The psychic said that she would give a refund for the session, and she promptly escorted Beth out. The implication seems to be that the psychic feared that she, too, would be cursed if she spent more time with Beth. Weatherly explains that Beth subsequently sought out a 'spiritual figure' for counselling and a blessing. After the latter, Beth's life began to get better.

**Case 8: A family death**

A person called Charles, living outside New Orleans, had a possible BEK encounter while heading home from a night out with friends (Weatherly, 2017, pp. 155-7). I say 'possible BEK encounter' because there's no explicit mention of black eyes in the undated report.

Charles had been dropped off at the end of the block and didn't have far to walk to his home. After he'd walked a few steps, someone called out. Charles turned round. A boy was close to him. Charles asked what he was doing out so late. Instead of answering, the boy suggested that Charles invite him to walk along with him. The boy's skin seemed very white, although that may have been an effect of the street lighting. At any rate, Charles felt afraid and walked off quickly, without responding to the boy's request. But he heard him saying that Charles would be sorry that he hadn't listened to him.

At 5 a.m., Charles was woken by a phone call from his mother, who had bad news: his seemingly healthy sister had died that night – of a heart attack in her sleep, according to the doctors. Right then, Charles's thoughts turned to the strange boy he'd encountered on the street. Later, when he told his mother about the boy, she surmised that Charles had been cursed. She retrieved her Bible and prayed over him. After some blessings, she got him to promise to read certain biblical passages during the week.

Charles experienced insomnia for weeks after the encounter. Fearing that he might encounter the strange boy again, he avoided walking along the block late at night. In relating his experience, he explained that he still read from the Bible each night.

Weatherly notes that Charles wasn't the only person to contact him regarding a death in their family after a BEK encounter.

**Comments**

In respect of Case 5, Weatherly (2017, p. 148) explains that he wasn't able to interview directly the son of Tom and Sharon. It's not clear whether he interviewed or corresponded with Tom, or whether Sharon was his sole informant about the alleged events.

To the extent that Cases 5-7 are unusual and not typical, it could be that the unhappy events following the BEK encounters were merely coincidental. However, in each case, they reportedly occurred *very soon* after the encounter, which gives credence to the notion that a curse was operative. In respect of Case 5, Tom wouldn't have been driving Sharon's car at the time of his accident if it hadn't been for Sharon's BEK encounter. Arguably, then, the BEK (or the intelligence behind it) played a causal role in the accident, and maybe in the strange illness that afflicted Tom and Sharon's son.

In Case 8, Charles's encounter with a strange child is said to have occurred around 2 a.m. He learned of his sister's death at 5 a.m. But since the precise time of her death isn't stated (and perhaps wasn't known), it's not clear whether she died *before* or *after* Charles encountered the boy in the street. If his sister died *before* Charles encountered the strange boy, her death was presumably not related to him, unless we assume that curses can work retroactively (i.e. backwards in time).

## THE NATURE OF BLACK-EYED CHILDREN

Like other allegedly paranormal manifestations, BEKs are open to different interpretations, not all mutually exclusive. In considering the nature of the phenomenon, it's worth noting that there are overlaps with other types of anomalous event. For example, the 'alien greys' who feature in reports of UFO close encounters and abductions are typically described as having black eyes, albeit of a different shape and size from those of BEKs.

Given their reported habit of disappearing very quickly, the behaviour of BEKs has an apparitional character. On the other hand, leaving aside fictional spectres, apparitions seldom speak to witnesses at length, and they don't require permission to enter buildings or vehicles.

As noted above, bad odours are sometimes noticed in the wake of BEK encounters. Unpleasant or repellent smells have also been reported in connection with bigfoot encounters.[5] Witnesses are likely to find the latter frightening. But intimidating behaviour by these creatures or entities seems to be aimed at protecting their territory – a wish to drive away intruders – and may not be indicative of malign intent. Indeed, there are accounts of bigfoots coming to the aid of humans. For example, Thom Powell (2003, pp. 145-6) mentions an instance related to him by a woman called Dora Bradley, who'd reportedly had a succession of bigfoot encounters in the vicinity of her childhood home in Montgomery County, Missouri. On the night in question, she was anxiously awaiting the arrival home of her father, who had an alcohol problem. She feared that he might have crashed his pick-up vehicle. Looking through a window, she saw him cradled in the arms of a bigfoot. The creature set him down and then disappeared. Her father was drunk. He'd had an accident and was in pain. His wrecked vehicle was subsequently found three miles away.

Regarding the contention that BEKs (or, at least, some BEKs) need permission to enter a home or vehicle, there's a parallel with vampire lore, since there's a tradition that vampires can't enter a home without permission.

## A genuine phenomenon or an 'urban legend'?

The aforementioned cases are intriguing. But leaving aside Case 1 (that of Brian Bethel), there's a high degree of anonymity about the alleged witnesses. And I'm not sure whether, and to what extent, there's been any corroboration of what they reported. Of course, if BEK encounters, by their very nature, tend to be single-witness events, the scope for corroboration is limited. But if a witness genuinely claims to have been upset by a BEK encounter, there might be family members or friends who could confirm that the witness told them of the experience around the time and seemed disturbed by it.

As I noted earlier in this chapter, it's been suggested that the BEK phenomenon isn't a paranormal one, but an 'urban legend' that's been propagated by the Internet. Even if some witness reports are genuine, they may have been generated by pranksters wearing black contact lenses. However, it seems that back in the 1990s, when stories about BEKs started circulating on the Internet, black contact lenses were expensive items and perhaps not easily available. Therefore, it's questionable whether children or adolescents would have gone to the expense and bother of acquiring them for one-off pranks.

So-called urban legends usually involve 'a friend of a friend' – someone distant from the person relating the tale. Weatherly (2017, p. 15) notes that, by contrast, it's easy to find people who've had BEK encounters. But I don't know whether that's the case in the UK, where I'm based. Although I've spoken to many people who've reported anomalous experiences, I can't remember any of them telling me of a personal BEK encounter.

Weatherly (*ibid.*, p. 15) states that while it's popular to relate urban legends, the majority of people who've had BEK encounters are extremely reluctant to talk about them. Perhaps he's right. But maybe some people who *haven't* had BEK encounters are quite happy to pretend that they have, drawing on stories on the Internet (perhaps themselves bogus) as templates for further BEK tales, thus perpetuating a myth.

## Demonic entities?

Judging from reports of BEK encounters – at least, those mentioned by Weatherly – it seems that witnesses are likely to find BEKs creepy, even before they notice that the entities have completely black eyes. Furthermore, as already noted, bad things may happen in the immediate wake of BEK encounters. Not surprisingly, then, one interpretation of the phenomenon is that BEKs are evil, demonic beings. A belief held in pre-Islamic Arabia, and continued in Islam, is that there's a race of mostly mischievous, or even malevolent, spirit beings. They're referred to as the *jinn* (or *djinn*). From this perspective, BEKs could be construed as jinn.

## Alien-human hybrids?

The alien abduction phenomenon was discussed briefly in Chapter 4. If we assume that the black-eyed 'alien greys' often mentioned in abduction reports are physically real, and if we further assume that an alien-human hybridization programme is underway, it could be that BEKs (or, at least, some of them) are human-alien hybrids. However, in itself, this notion doesn't explain what BEKs are up to when they interact with humans.

## Apparitions or materializations?

Although BEKs may *seem* to display a degree of physicality – for example, by knocking on doors – it could be that they're essentially hallucinatory. Certainly, as I noted previously, accounts suggest that they can move from one spot to another, multiply, or disappear, within a very short space of time. In Case 3, the witness was reportedly able to see *through* the black-eyed figure he was seeing.

If BEKs *are* hallucinatory, that doesn't entitle us to infer that nothing paranormal is involved. Assuming that the witnesses weren't suffering from a morbid susceptibility to auditory and visual hallucinations, their experiences could be seen as paranormally-engendered hallucinations. By the same token, the repeated sighting of a ghost in a haunted house could be both paranormal *and* hallucinatory.

Another possibility is that BEK encounters – or some of them – involve *transient materializations*. In other words, BEKs may have a degree of physicality, but only briefly, rather like the 'spirit forms' that manifest during séances with physical mediums.

It could be that BEKs are 'thought-forms' or 'tulpas', unwittingly created by humans. Imagine, for instance, that we share a collective subconscious mind, and that it can respond to widespread collective wishes by creating manifestations to satisfy them. For example, if there's a widespread wish to hear exciting reports of the Loch Ness Monster, the collective subconscious mind could perhaps produce transient materializations of 'Nessie'. By the same token, if numerous people read excitingly creepy tales of BEKs on the Internet and want to hear more such stories, could it be that their collective wish brings about BEK sightings? The witnesses themselves might have no wish for such experiences, but they could be heavily 'outvoted' by those who want it to happen!

Another possibility is that such paranormal displays aren't orchestrated by a collective subconscious mind, but rather by some sort of external higher intelligence. In my view, it's not necessary to assume that such an intelligence is extraterrestrial, 'interdimensional' or from the future. It may have always been with us, but largely hiding in the shadows.

In terms of this notion, I think we should beware of what I term the 'plurality fallacy' – the assumption that if someone sees, for example, three aliens, three ghosts, or three BEKs, that three entities are actually involved. Instead, there could be just one intelligent agent behind the whole performance. By way of analogy, imagine that visitors to an art gallery are looking at a painting by a famous artist, and that it depicts two men and a woman. A tour guide asks one of them, 'What do you see there?' The person responds, 'Three people – two men and a woman.' That would be incorrect, because the visitor would actually be seeing just *one* thing – a painting, created by one person!

## 'Feeding off fear'

Witnesses tend to find spontaneous paranormal phenomena perplexing and frightening, and it has been suggested that what's behind them 'feeds off' this fear. In their 2014 book *Contagion*, which deals with poltergeist and haunt phenomena, Darren Ritson and Mike Hallowell discuss this possibility. Weatherly (2017, pp. 87-9) refers to the notion of 'hungry ghosts' in Chinese religion and culture. According to this tradition, a discarnate spirit might attempt to frighten someone, and feed off the resulting emotions. In BEK encounters, witnesses typically, if not invariably, feel afraid, both during the encounter itself and for a time afterwards. Are these events orchestrated to enable some sort of paranormal intelligence to feed off the resultant fear?

Although the notion of 'feeding off fear' may have some validity, I must admit that I find it somewhat hard to grasp, because fear is a mental and physiological *state*, not a physical substance. But perhaps 'feeding off fear' should be understood figuratively rather than literally. Imagine, for instance, that the intelligence behind BEK encounters is cruel and sadistic. If so, it may find it gratifying to scare the wits out of witnesses, if only to demonstrate to itself that it has the power to do so. It's not a pleasant thought!

# CHAPTER 7

# FAMILY CURSES

In this chapter, I'll consider the question of whether families or different generations of families might be cursed. The notion of a family curse is sometimes invoked to explain a disproportionate amount of bad luck that certain families attract. The cases we tend to hear about usually involve high-profile families, such as the Kennedys in the USA. In truth, it may be near impossible to say for sure that any given family has experienced significantly more misfortune than might be expected by chance, not least because information about unhappiness or loss in people's lives won't always be made public.

Imagine, for example, that a woman – let's call her Mary – has experienced episodes of severe depression in her life, and that she's sometimes contemplated suicide. Further, imagine that she and her family are very 'private people'. If so, information about her problems might never come to the attention of people outside her family. Contrast this with the situation of someone else – let's call her Judy – who's very open about the ups and downs in her life, and who frequently posts information about them on her social media pages. From this, people might wrongly infer that Judy has experienced more unhappiness in her life than Mary.

There doesn't seem to be any 'cosmic' law stipulating that unhappy events will be evenly distributed across the human population. Purely by chance, it's only to be expected that some people will be luckier or less lucky than others. And even if it seems that members of an extended family, or different generations of it, have experienced a lot of misfortune, there could well be plausible prosaic explanations, obviating the need to bring in the speculative notion of a curse.

When I started working on this chapter, I was hoping to include more examples of presumed family curses. However, in researching such stories, I was sometimes left unsure about the accuracy of the historical details. For example, it's been claimed that in the 16th century, John Erskine, the first Earl of Mar, incurred the anger of an abbot, who uttered a curse or prediction concerning the Erskine family. The first earl himself didn't personally experience any of the predicted misfortune, but later generations did. However, among other things, I'm not sure whether there ever was a curse in the first place. Maybe the story of the curse was a later invention. Therefore, to minimize historical uncertainties, I've chosen to discuss relatively recent cases.

## THE 'KENNEDY CURSE'

The Kennedy family in the USA has had a long history of involvement in business, politics, and other activities. Of course, I'm not referring to everyone there named Kennedy, but to those with close or fairly close ties to the late President John F. Kennedy (whom I'll henceforth refer to, for brevity, with the well-known abbreviation *JFK*). Like JFK himself, quite a number of other prominent Kennedys have met untimely deaths or misfortune, giving rise to the notion that the family is cursed. In a televised statement in 1969 concerning the death of Mary Jo Kopechne (see below), Senator Ted Kennedy speculated that maybe there really was such a curse.

In the interests of clarity, I'll refer to different generations of the family, starting with a couple who emigrated from Ireland to the USA in 1849. I shan't go into details about everyone belonging to each respective generation. Instead, I'll focus on prominent Kennedys, and particularly those who met untimely deaths or who experienced significant misfortune.

### First generation

Patrick Kennedy and his wife-to-be, Bridget, hailed from County Wexford in the south-east of Ireland. They moved to Massachusetts in 1849, marrying later that same year. They lived in East Boston. Patrick, who worked as a cooper (barrel maker), died of cholera in his mid-thirties. The disease was rife in the local area, so we don't need to attribute his death to a curse. His widow (the great-grandmother of JFK) died in 1888, aged about 67.

### Second generation

Patrick and Bridget had five children: two sons, and three daughters. The elder son died of cholera as an infant. His younger brother, Patrick Joseph ('P. J. Kennedy') had a prominent career in business and politics.

## Third generation

P.J. Kennedy's son Joseph (known as 'Joseph P. Kennedy Sr') married Rose Fitzgerald, the eldest daughter of the mayor of Boston. Joseph went on to become a chairman of the US Securities and Exchange Commission and a US ambassador to the UK.

## Fourth generation

Joseph and Rose had nine children. I'll mention seven of them (in order of their dates of birth), since they either died relatively young or experienced major problems.

*Joseph P. Kennedy Jr*

Joseph, born in 1915, was killed in 1944 when two on board explosions of unknown cause destroyed a military aircraft that he was piloting.

*JFK*

JFK was born in 1917. As the candidate of the Democratic Party, he narrowly beat his Republican rival, Richard Nixon, in the 1960 presidential election, becoming the 35th president of the USA in January 1961. It was during his presidency that the Cuban Missile Crisis arose. This was arguably one of the most critical times in the Cold War. The crisis was defused via skilful negotiations with Cuba's ally, the Soviet Union. But on 22 November 1963, JFK was assassinated in Dallas, Texas. Officially, his death was attributed to a 'lone gunman', Lee Harvey Oswald, who was himself fatally shot by a man called Jack Ruby on 24 November. There's been much debate and controversy about JFK's assassination, with many theories being advanced.

JFK is well known to have been an adulterer, and he's rumoured to have had a relationship with the actress, model, and singer Marilyn Monroe (1926-62). However, it has been suggested that this may have amounted, at the very most, to a one-night stand.[1]

*Rose Kennedy*

Born in 1918, Rose incurred brain damage as a result of inadequate obstetric care. She subsequently exhibited mental deficiency, convulsions, and behavioural problems. These were an embarrassment to her high-achieving family – or, at least, to her father, Joseph – and she was subjected to non-consensual brain surgery (a lobotomy) when she was 23. Far from curing or ameliorating her problems, it left her unable to walk or talk.[2] She died of natural causes, aged 86, having spent most of her life in institutions of one sort or another.

*Kathleen Kennedy*

Kathleen Kennedy, born in 1920, had close friends in London. She married a British aristocrat, who was killed on military service in Belgium four months after their wedding. Later, she had a relationship with another British aristocrat, a married man. He and Kathleen died in a plane crash in May 1948.

*Patricia Kennedy*

Patricia Kennedy, born in 1924, married a British actor, Peter Lawford, with whom she had four children. She battled alcoholism and cancer of the tongue, and died of pneumonia in 2006.

*Robert ('Bobby') Kennedy*

Robert Kennedy, born in 1925, was the USA's Attorney General between 1961 and 1964. He and his wife Ethel were married in 1950 and had a very large family. Robert served as a US Senator and entered the campaign for the presidential election in 1968. But in June of that year, he was fatally shot in Los Angeles. A Palestinian militant called Sirhan Sirhan was found guilty of the murder and remains in prison, although he has recently (August 2021) been recommended for parole. The assertion that he fired the fatal shots has been disputed.

Like his elder brother JFK and his younger brother Edward, Bobby Kennedy is reputed to have been an adulterer. He was reportedly involved with Marilyn Monroe, and it has even been suggested that he murdered her.[3]

*Edward ('Ted') Kennedy*

Edward Kennedy, born in 1932, became a US Senator in 1962. He was seriously injured in a plane crash in 1964. He and his wife, known as Joan, had three children. Their marriage was turbulent and ended in divorce. Edward subsequently remarried and had a further two children. He died of a brain tumour in 2009.

On a night in July 1969, Ted Kennedy was involved in an accident that cost the life of a 28-year-old woman, Mary Jo Kopechne. They were in his car when it plunged from a bridge into water. Kennedy extricated himself from the vehicle and reportedly attempted, unsuccessfully, to save his companion. But there was a delay of some nine or ten hours before he reported the incident to the authorities. If he had done so immediately, Kopechne might have survived.

## Fifth generation

Leaving aside a miscarriage and stillbirth, JFK and his wife Jacqueline had three children, one of whom, a son, died after just two days. The other son, John Fitzgerald Kennedy Jr, was killed in a plane crash in 1999 along with his wife, Carolyn, and sister-in-law, Lauren. He'd been piloting the private aircraft. Keith McCloskey discusses this case in some detail in his 2020 book *Unsolved Aviation Mysteries* (pp. 64-96).

Bobby Kennedy and his wife, Ethel, had 11 children. In August 1973, a Jeep driven by their eldest son, Joseph P. Kennedy II, overturned. One of the passengers, Joseph's brother, David, suffered a fractured vertebra, and the latter's girlfriend, Pam Kelley, was permanently paralyzed, spending the rest of her life in a wheelchair. The aforementioned David died from drug poisoning in 1984. Bobby and Ethel's fourth son, Michael, was fatally injured after hitting a tree in a skiing accident in 1997 at Aspen Mountain, Colorado. He wasn't wearing a helmet. Mary Richardson Kennedy, an ex-wife of Bobby Kennedy's son Robert Jr, reportedly had substance abuse problems, and committed suicide, by hanging, in 2012.

Ted Kennedy's eldest child was called Kara. She was successfully treated for lung cancer, but she died of a heart attack in 2011 at the relatively young age of 51. At the age of 12, Ted Kennedy's second child, Edward Jr, was diagnosed with osteosarcoma (a type of bone cancer) in his right leg. The affected limb was amputated.

Christopher Lawford, a son of Patricia Kennedy (one of JFK's sisters, mentioned above), had a history of substance abuse and died of a heart attack in 2018 at the age of 63.

## Sixth and seventh generations

The fifth of Bobby Kennedy's 11 children was Mary (known by her second name, Courtney). Her daughter Saoirse Kennedy Hill, who had a history of depression, died of a drug overdose (deemed to have been accidental) in 2019. She was only 22.[4]

The eldest of Bobby Kennedy's children was Kathleen. Her daughter Maeve Fahey Kennedy McKean and the latter's eight-year-old son Gideon went missing in Chesapeake Bay, Maryland, on 2 April 2020. It appears that they may have set out in a small canoe to retrieve a ball that had landed in the water, and that they were then swept out into the bay by high winds. Maeve's body was recovered on 6 April 2020, and that of her son two days later.

## Comments

It's not just the Kennedys themselves who've had bad luck. Some of the people related to them through marriage have experienced misfortune. For example, Bobby Kennedy's wealthy in-laws, George and Ann Skakel, were killed when a private aircraft they were travelling in crashed in Oklahoma in October 1955. And along with three others, their son, George Jr (a brother-in-law of Bobby Kennedy) was killed in the crash of a private plane in Idaho in 1966. His widow died the following year after choking on a piece of meat at her home in Connecticut.

JFK's wife Jaqueline was sitting beside her husband when he was fatally shot in 1963. Five years later, she married the Greek business mogul Aristotle Onassis, although the latter's son and daughter, Alexander and Christina (from his first marriage), were reportedly unhappy about the union. Alexander was a passenger in his personal amphibious plane when it crashed at Hellinikon International Airport in Athens in January 1973. He died of his injuries the next day, aged only 24. Christina also died young, at the age of 38 in 1988, apparently of natural causes. Despite her wealth, she had a turbulent life, with four marriages that ended in divorce, and problems with her weight, depression, and drug dependence. Her mother had died of a suspected drug overdose in 1974.

As noted, quite a few Kennedys or people related to them have died in plane crashes. But it should be borne in mind that nearly all of these deaths involved private aircraft. Statistics indicate that private flying is riskier than commercial flying.[5] It's largely the preserve of the wealthy or relatively wealthy, and the aforementioned plane crashes occurred years ago, when such flying was more hazardous than it is nowadays.[6] In other words, these deaths in aviation accidents may reflect prosaic factors rather than the operation of a curse.

When people of limited means have large families, it's generally a passport for poverty and overcrowded living conditions. Some of the aforementioned Kennedys had large families. But they were, of course, wealthy. Nevertheless, with so many children, it's only to be expected, statistically speaking, that there would have been more tragic deaths than in smaller families. Furthermore, if families contain very high achievers, some of those who don't reach the same dizzying heights might have feelings of inadequacy. It's not hard to imagine that this could result in people seeking solace through excessive drinking or drug use, perhaps leading to accidental overdoses or suicides.

As leading politicians, JFK and Bobby Kennedy would have had enemies. In the case of JFK, for instance, these may have included elements within parts of the US power structure (e.g. the CIA) as well as outsiders, such as the Mafia and Cuban exiles who felt that he wasn't doing enough to overthrow the regime of Fidel Castro in Cuba.

## THE END OF THE ROMANOV DYNASTY

The Romanov dynasty ruled the Russian empire for around 400 years. The last Romanov tsar (emperor) was Nicholas II (1868-1918), a first cousin of the UK's George V. There was tragedy from the outset of his reign. A public banquet was arranged in Moscow to celebrate his coronation in 1896. In response to a rumour that food and beer were running short at the front, the crowd surged forward, with people being crushed and trampled. There were reportedly nearly 1,400 deaths on the spot, and no doubt other people died later of their injuries. The new emperor and his wife, Alexandra (a German-born princess), were distraught when they heard the news. But they were obliged to attend a ball that night at the residence of the French ambassador, which the public mistook as indicating indifference to what had occurred earlier that day.

The tsar and his wife were under pressure to have a son, since a male heir was required to continue the Romanov dynasty. But the first four of their five children were daughters, and their son, Alexei, suffered from haemophilia, a potentially life-threatening illness at the time. In desperation, the empress sought help from Grigori Rasputin (1869-1916), a Siberian-born man of humble origins who presented himself as a mystic and holy man. Alexandra became convinced that Rasputin had healing powers, and he acquired considerable prestige and influence within the royal household. However, this was resented by some senior officials and sections of the general public, who distrusted or despised him. He was murdered in 1916.

Alexandra herself was very unpopular among the tsar's Russian subjects. She was shy and introverted, which was interpreted as indicative of coldness and arrogance, and when the First World War broke out, her German background wouldn't have helped to endear her to the public. The monarchy was swept aside in the Bolshevik revolution of February 1917. On the night of 16/17 July 1918, Nicholas, his wife, and five children were executed in Yekaterinburg (also known as Ekaterinburg) in the Ural region of Russia. Some of their retainers were also killed that night. Whether the order for the executions came from the Ural Regional Soviet or from 'the top' (Lenin and his senior Bolshevik associates) seems unclear. The Russian Civil War was underway at the time. On one side were the Bolshevik communists (the 'Reds'), who eventually prevailed. The opposing 'White' forces were made up of people of disparate views (monarchists, democratic socialists, nationalists, etc.), perhaps united by little more than their opposition to the Bolsheviks.

## Comments

While the fate of the Romanovs has elements of tragedy, the notion that they were the victims of a curse doesn't seem very credible. Arguably, the fall of the tsardom had more to do with broad social, political, and economic changes sweeping across much of Europe around that time. For example, the French monarchy had gone by the end of the 18th century, and within just a few months of the executions at Yekaterinburg, Germany would lose the First World War and become a republic. Also, as noted, the tsar and his wife didn't enjoy universal affection and support from the Russian public.

## THE GRIMALDI FAMILY

In medieval times, the Grimaldis were one of the ruling families in what we now call Italy. They rose to power through the Crusades and by capturing Genoa in north-west Italy. Nowadays, they're best known for being the rulers of Monaco, which Rainier I (c. 1267-1314) and his army captured in 1297. Whether true or not, Rainier is said to have kidnapped a young woman, who subsequently became a witch and put a curse on the Grimaldis.

In fairly recent times, Prince Rainier III married the American actress Grace Kelly (1929-82). They had two daughters and a son: Caroline (b. 1957), Albert (b. 1958), and Stéphanie (b. 1965).

While driving with Stéphanie to a railway station, Grace missed a sharp turn, and the car went down a 120-foot slope. Stéphanie survived the accident with relatively minor injuries. Her sister Caroline informed the author Jeffrey Robinson that their mother, in a panic, kept saying that she couldn't stop, and that the brakes weren't working. Stéphanie tried pulling on the handbrake, but it didn't stop the car.[7]

The mother and daughter were rushed to a hospital. Grace had suffered a cerebral haemorrhage, probably caused by the accident, and didn't regain consciousness. Her situation was hopeless, and the life support machine sustaining her was turned off the following day, at her husband's request. She was 52.

In an interview, Stéphanie explained that her mother had complained of a headache and then seemed to black out for a moment, whereupon the car swerved before going down the slope. It's thought that the crash was caused by Grace having a 'cerebral vascular incident' (this may be a reference to a type of mini-stroke known as a *transient ischaemic attack*), and that she confused the car's brake pedal with the accelerator, or that she lost the use of her legs.

Rainier III died at the age of 81 in 2005 of a lung condition related to his heavy smoking.

Caroline (the elder daughter of Grace and Rainier) has been married three times. There were no children from her first marriage, which ended in divorce. The marriage was eventually annulled by the Catholic Church. She had three children from her second marriage, which ended when her husband died in a powerboat racing accident at the age of 30. By her current husband, Ernst August, whom she married in 1999, she had a daughter. Ernst is nominally the head of the House of Hanover. However, the Kingdom of Hanover came to an end in 1866 when it was annexed by Prussia. Caroline and Ernst have reportedly separated.

Albert (Grace and Rainier's son) is married with two children by his wife. But he has faced paternity claims regarding other children.

Stéphanie (Grace and Rainier's younger daughter) had two children by her bodyguard, whom she went on to marry, although the marriage didn't last long. She then had a third child by her head of security, whom she didn't marry. There were no children from a brief second marriage.

## Comments

While the death of Grace Kelly can be seen as tragic, there seems little reason to think that it was related to a curse rather than natural causes. Among prominent, wealthy people there's often quite a high number of divorces and a high turnover of partners. Therefore, comparatively speaking, there may be nothing particularly exceptional about the private lives of the son and daughters of Rainier and Grace. Furthermore, a high turnover of partners or spouses may not be an entirely reliable guide to the amount of unhappiness and stress that wealthy, high-profile people experience.

## THE NEPALESE MONARCHY

There's a curse story about the Nepalese royal family, based on an incident that allegedly occurred about 250 years ago when the first Nepalese king took the throne. However, I don't know whether it's anything more than fanciful folklore. A guru supposedly spat out or vomited up some food and then asked the king to eat it. Not surprisingly, he declined to do so. The guru then proclaimed that because of this lack of respect and humility, the monarchy would last for only 10 generations.

In June 2001, there was a mass shooting at the royal palace in Kathmandu, Nepal's capital. The king and queen and seven other members of the royal family were killed. Then, Eton-educated Crown Prince Dipendra reportedly shot himself in the head. He died in hospital three days later without regaining consciousness. A government inquiry named him as the perpetrator of the palace massacre, although that assertion has been disputed. Prior to his death, while he was in a coma, he was declared the new king. His uncle,

Gyanendra then became the monarch and remained so until 2008, when Nepal became a federal republic. Gyanendra had briefly been the king before, in the early 1950s. He was still a child then, and other members of the family had gone into exile in India.

## Comments

I'm not sure whether it's true to say that the Nepalese monarchy spanned exactly 10 generations. That might be hard to calculate precisely. Gyanendra's second (2001-8) reign would have to be disregarded, since although a king might reign twice, he would belong to only one generation of his family. If the story about the guru is true, and if the monarchy did span 10 generations, the guru's pronouncement could be interpreted as an accurate prophecy rather than a curse that influenced the course of Nepal's subsequent history. If it happens to be the case that the Nepalese monarchy spanned 10 generations, it could simply be a matter of chance. Arguably, the ending of the monarchy in Nepal in 2008 had more to do with the fraught political situation – widespread discontent with the monarchy and a Maoist insurgency – than with a curse.

# CHAPTER 8

# CURSES IN THE MUSIC AND FILM INDUSTRIES

There are stories of curses, or assumed curses, in the music and film industries. While of interest in their own right, they deserve to be considered in a cool-headed and critical manner. Some of them, at least, appear to be nothing more than fanciful myths or legends. It's not always clear who, or what, did the alleged cursing, or what purpose the supposed curse served, or continues to serve. In some cases, the inference of a curse stems from nothing more than a seemingly unusual distribution or number of events. The following is a selection of examples.

### THE '27 CLUB'

It's been suggested that a disproportionate number of popular musicians, artists, or actors have died, of one cause or another, at the early age of 27. Regarding singers and musicians, well-known 'members' of this so-called '27 Club' have included:

*Kurt Cobain* (1967-94), an American singer, songwriter, and guitarist with the grunge rock band Nirvana. He committed suicide in Seattle at the age of 27.

*Jimi Hendrix* (1942-70), an American guitarist, vocalist, and songwriter. He asphyxiated on his vomit in a drug-related incident in London at the age of 27.

*Brian Jones* (1942-69), a British multi-instrumentalist, songwriter, and founder member of the Rolling Stones. He drowned, in disputed circumstances, in the swimming pool of his East Sussex home at the age of 27.

*Janis Joplin* (1943-70), an American blues and rock singer-songwriter. She died, aged 27, from an accidental heroin overdose in Hollywood, California.

*Jim Morrison* (1943-71), an American singer-songwriter and frontman with the Doors. He died in Paris, aged 27, of heart failure or, possibly, a heroin overdose.

*Amy Winehouse* (1983-2011), a British singer-songwriter. She died in London of alcohol poisoning at the age of 27.

However, many other performers have died young, or relatively young, but *not* at the age of 27. For example, Buddy Holly (1933-56) was 22 when he was killed in an aircraft crash in Iowa, along with 17-year-old Ritchie Valens (of 'La Bamba' fame) and 28-year-old J.P. 'the Big Bopper' Richardson. Ex-Beatle John Lennon was 40 when he was fatally shot by a deranged fan in New York City. John Bonham, the drummer with Led Zeppelin, was 32 when he asphyxiated on his vomit after consuming a prodigious amount of vodka. Similarly, Keith Moon, the drummer with The Who, was 32 when he also asphyxiated on his vomit.

A study published in the *British Medical Journal* in 2011 found that 'famous musicians'[1] in their 20s and 30s were two to three times more likely to experience a premature death than members of the general UK population (no doubt because of their risky lifestyles).[2,3] The researchers found a very small blip in risk at the age of 27. But there were very similar blips for the ages of 25 and 32. Therefore, if people want to believe in a '27 Club', they also need to believe in a '25 Club' and a '32 Club'! Even if the study had found a marked peak in deaths at the age of 27, it wouldn't have necessarily meant that a malign paranormal force or curse was behind them. Adrian Barnett, the lead researcher of the aforementioned study, acknowledged that there were a couple of possible reasons why deaths at 27 might be more common, one being that rock musicians tend to become famous in their early twenties, with their risk-taking (via drugs, alcohol, or reckless behaviour) steadily increasing from there and peaking four to five years later. The other possibility he mentioned was that musicians who know about the '27 Club' might, consciously or unconsciously, behave more dangerously at that age, even being drawn into committing suicide then. However, as noted, the study didn't find a marked peak in deaths at the age of 27.

## STORIES INVOLVING JIMMY PAGE

Middlesex-born Jimmy Page became a session guitarist in his teens, and eventually became a member of the Yardbirds. In 1968, he put together a band called Led Zeppelin, which initially and briefly toured as the New Yardbirds. It was a four-member outfit, with Page on lead guitar. John Paul Jones (originally John Richard Baldwin) played bass guitar (and, at times, other instruments). John Bonham was the drummer, and Robert Plant was the lead vocalist. The Yardbirds started as a blues-based group, and much of Led Zeppelin's music had a bluesy flavour. Indeed, some of their recorded album tracks were re-workings of songs by black blues musicians, although the band also produced tracks with a folk music character. Deservedly or not, they soon became one of the most successful rock groups in the world, if not *the* most successful.

### Interest the occult

Page, who was born in 1944, developed a fascination with the occultist Aleister Crowley (1875-1947) and acquired Crowley memorabilia. In 1970, he bought Boleskine House, an extensive bungalow located beside Loch Ness in Scotland. Crowley had owned it between 1899 and 1913, and had reportedly carried out magical rituals there. But I don't know whether Page followed suit. Indeed, although he owned the house for some 11 or 12 years, he spent relatively little time there.

Crowley was born into a wealthy Plymouth Brethren family as Edward Alexander Crowley. He attended private schools and then Trinity College, Cambridge, which he left without a degree. He inherited a small family fortune at an early age, enabling him to pursue his interests. He rejected his parents' Christian fundamentalist beliefs and was drawn to 'Western esotericism'. He founded his own religion, called 'Thelema', and led a colourful life, which included mountaineering, writing (pornographic poetry, for instance), affairs with members of both sexes, and the use of sex, drugs, and magic (which Crowley preferred to spell as 'magick') in an attempt to attain altered states of consciousness. He was described as the 'wickedest man in the world' and he ended his life as a heroin addict. His libertine lifestyle gave him cachet with the hippy generation, no doubt facilitated by his appearing, along with others, on the cover of the Beatles' seminal 1967 album, *Sgt Pepper's Lonely Hearts Club Band*.

A vague rumour, perhaps no more than a groundless myth, is that Jimmy Page, propelled by his interest in the occult, persuaded two fellow members of Led Zeppelin – the singer, Robert Plant, and the drummer, John Bonham – to join him in summoning occult powers to bring Led Zeppelin success. According to this story, the bassist, John Paul Jones, declined to enter the arrangement. If dabbling with the occult attracts negative consequences, this presumed 'Faustian pact' could be seen as having a bearing on the drummer's early death and a tragedy that ensued in Plant's life (both mentioned below). However, even if three members of Led Zeppelin did call on occult forces or entities to enhance the band's prospects, that may have had no bearing on what subsequently happened to them.

## The Kenneth Anger curse

In his book *Jimmy Page: The Definitive Biography*, the music journalist Chris Salewicz explains that Page attended a Sotheby's auction in 1973 and bidded for a pornographic manuscript by Aleister Crowley. Another bidder was Kenneth Anger (originally Kenneth Wilbur Anglemyer), a Californian underground experimental filmmaker, actor, and author. He was born in 1927 and was (and perhaps still is) an adherent of Thelema, the religion that Crowley founded. Page and Anger got talking and became friends. At the time, Anger had been working for several years on a short film, *Lucifer Rising*, and was anxious to obtain suitable music for it, which Page agreed to provide. However, in the second half of 1976, the men's relationship broke down. There may have been several reasons. Salewicz (p. 348-9) notes:

> Anger decried the guitarist for time-wasting and lack of dedication to the project, and claimed that Page's personal problems – code for his heroin habit – had made him impossible to work with. Page had supposedly been working on the film for the past three years, but at the point Anger spoke out against him had delivered only 28 minutes of completed tape.[4]

Salewicz doesn't specify the precise length of soundtrack that Anger asked Page to provide. During an interview in 1977, Page told Salewicz that the footage of the film needed to be put together before the music could be added, and that Anger had failed to keep in touch with him about it.

In the event, Anger didn't use Page's material in his film; and he supposedly put a curse on Page and his then-girlfriend, Charlotte Martin, although I don't know precisely when that was. Salewicz (pp. 352-3) states:

> The 'Kenneth Anger curse' [...] was no idle threat. Almost 30 years later, a still-angry Anger confirmed that he had indeed followed through with it. 'He [Page] was a multi-millionaire miser,' he said. 'He and Charlotte, they had so many servants, yet they would never offer me a cup of tea or a sandwich. Which is such a mistake on their part because I put the curse of King Midas on them. If you're greedy and just amass gold you'll get an illness. So I turned her and Jimmy Page into statues of gold.'
>
> Page was utterly dismissive of this. He told me later that this 'curse' consisted of newspaper cuttings underlined in red ink that Anger sent to him. 'It was quite pathetic, actually. *Lucifer Rising* was going to be a masterpiece, but he didn't manage to pull it off.'

It would be interesting to know whether the curse entailed more than that. Did Anger engage in some sort of ritual aimed at hurting Page and Charlotte, or was it simply a matter of his wishing them misfortune? As noted, he referred to turning them into statues of gold. Was that just a figure of speech, or did he actually create gold effigies of them?

In fact, things had started going wrong for Led Zeppelin even before Page and Anger fell out. In August 1975, on the Greek island of Rhodes, a car being driven by Robert Plant's wife shot off the road and struck a tree after she misjudged a bend. She, her husband, and their two children all suffered significant injuries. Jimmy Page's daughter Scarlet was a passenger in the car, but she survived relatively unscathed. Robert Plant incurred broken bones in his right leg and ankle, and also a fractured right elbow. Naturally, this disrupted Led Zeppelin's activities for a period.

Things got worse for Led Zeppelin. In July 1977, Robert Plant's five-year-old son, Zarac, died of a mysterious stomach virus while Plant was on tour with the band in the United States. And, in 1980, the group's drummer, John Bonham, died after inhaling his vomit following a heavy drinking binge. That effectively brought Led Zeppelin to an end, although the remaining group members did play together on occasions after that. However, as I've said, Anger's curse was supposedly directed at Page and his girlfriend, not other members of Led Zeppelin.

Page's post-Led Zeppelin years may not have brought as much success as when the group were at their height. But these things are relative. For example, even though his 1988 solo album, *Outrider*, wasn't universally acclaimed, it sold hundreds of thousands of copies. Indeed, in some respects, Page seems to have enjoyed good luck. For example, according to Salewicz's book, after being found in possession of cocaine in 1982, Page was given a conditional discharge, and after being caught again with the drug, in 1984, which would usually attract a jail sentence, he got away with just a modest fine.

## Did Page curse Eddie & the Hot Rods?

The rock group Eddie & the Hot Rods was formed in Essex in 1975. 'Eddie' was the name given to a dummy that featured prominently in the band's early gigs before being discarded. The group still exists.[5] But its line-up has undergone numerous changes over the years, with none of the original members remaining. Until his death in 2019, the singer, Barrie Masters, had been the only constant member.[6]

Their biggest hit was a pop-rock single titled 'Do Anything You Wanna Do'. It was written by Ed Hollis (the band's then-manager) and Graeme Douglas (a guitarist with the group). Released in the summer of 1977, under a shortened version of the band's name (the 'Rods')', it reached No. 9 in the British singles chart in September of that year. Its title was based on Aleister Crowley's dictum, 'Do what thou wilt shall be the whole of the law.' A picture of Crowley was put on the cover; and, to add a light touch, Hollis adorned the occultist's visage with a pair of Mickey Mouse ears.

It's rumoured that Jimmy Page put a curse on the band for this light-hearted treatment of Crowley. But I don't know whether Page has ever confirmed that. At any rate, from then on, the group experienced a succession of problems, such as being dropped by their recording label, and Hollis becoming addicted to heroin, and eventually dying from an overdose of the drug.

Paul Gray was the group's bassist when they recorded 'Do Anything You Wanna Do'. He told journalist Peter Watts that: 'Weird shit happened after that. A lot of people said we shouldn't have fucked about with Crowley.'[7] In March 2021, I contacted Gray, via a website, hoping that he might elaborate about the 'weird shit' that he'd referred to. He kindly responded, but indicated that he'd prefer to 'let this one lie now', although he was inclined to agree with my suggestion that even if Jimmy Page did curse Eddie & the Hot Rods, there's no way of telling whether it played any role in their difficulties, since with the music business being what it is, having a hit single is no guarantee of enduring stardom and good fortune.

I would have liked to ask Jimmy Page whether he and two other Led Zeppelin members tried to use occult means to enhance the band's success. I would also have liked to ask him whether he did indeed curse Eddie & the Hot Rods. Via the website of a PR company that acts for Page, I left a message, asking whether I could put some questions to him. Unfortunately, I received no reply.

## ROBERT JOHNSON AND THE 'CROSSROADS' CURSE

Robert Johnson (1911-38) was a black American blues guitarist, singer and songwriter, whose music influenced later musicians, such as Bob Dylan and Britain's Eric Clapton, Peter Green, Brian Jones, Mick Jagger and Robert Plant. It seems that his short life hasn't been well-documented, with even the cause of his death at 27 being unclear, although that age, if correct, makes him a member of the aforementioned '27 Club'. But there's uncertainty about the precise year of his birth. Therefore, it could be that he wasn't actually 27 when he died. It's possible that he was suffering from congenital syphilis or was deliberately poisoned. Such uncertainties about his life and death have no doubt created a fertile ground for myth and legend, with one story being that he sold his soul to the devil (or possibly struck a deal with a trickster god of African origin called Legba) to be granted musical success.[8]

'Cross Road Blues' (also known as 'Crossroads'), a blues song written and recorded by Johnson, became part of the mythology surrounding him, and supposedly referred to where he sold his soul to the Devil in exchange for his musical prowess. However, the lyrics of the song don't justify that fanciful interpretation. It's been suggested that the song is 'cursed', the evidence being that various people who've produced cover versions of it have experienced tragedies in their lives. For example, before he became a member of the group Cream, Eric Clapton got together with some other musicians and recorded a version of the song. Then, in 1968, Cream itself recorded 'Crossroads'. On 20 March 1991, Clapton's four-year-old son Conor accidentally fell to his death from an open window of an apartment on the 53rd floor of a building in New York City. He was playing hide-and-seek with his nanny. Unfortunately, the window's huge glass had been slid open by a janitor for cleaning, and the child fell through the open space.[9] But this was well over 20 years after Cream recorded 'Crossroads'. Therefore, to link Conor's death with his father's former involvement with the song seems very speculative.

## FLEETWOOD MAC: HIGH TURNOVER OF GUITARISTS?

Fleetwood Mac, formed in 1967, started out, essentially, as a blues group. It has undergone many changes in personnel over the years, with the drummer, Mick Fleetwood, being the only original member. It soon moved away from its early blues sound in the direction of rock, pop-rock, and folk-rock. It's seen a supposedly high turnover of guitarists, leading to speculation that something mysterious has been going on. But given that Fleetwood Mac has been in existence, in one form or another, for more than half a century, I suspect there's no real mystery here at all – just the expected comings and goings related to the ups and downs of life, such as mental and physical health problems, interpersonal tensions, and differing musical ambitions.

## THE CURSE OF THE NINTH (SYMPHONY)

Turning to classical and post-classical music, there's a superstition (and apparently no more than that) that a ninth symphony is somehow destined to be the person's last – that a composer will either die while writing it, or afterwards, but before completing a tenth. For example, the German composer Ludwig van Beethoven (1770-1827) died after writing his ninth symphony. However, numerous composers have, in fact, penned more than nine symphonies, including Andrzej Panufnik (1914-91), a Pole, whose creations included 10 symphonies, and the Finnish composer Kalevi Ensio Aho (b. 1949), whose output includes 17 symphonies.

## CURSED FILMS

A number of well-known films have had bad luck associated with them, leading to suggestions that a (Type II) curse has been at work. As always, though, one has to ask whether other factors played a role, or whether the misfortune was simply a matter of random bad luck. The following are some examples.

### *The Conqueror* (released in 1956)

This film, released in February 1956, starred John Wayne (1907-79) as Temüjin, a Mongol chief who came to be known as Ghengis Khan. Although it did fairly well at the box office, takings didn't match the outlays, and the production company, RKO Radio Pictures, subsequently went out of business. The film was a critical flop and has been described as one of the worst films of the period.

Much of the filming occurred near the city of St George in south-western Utah. Being downwind from the Nevada Test Site (originally known as the 'Nevada Proving Grounds'), where above-ground nuclear tests occurred between 1951 and 1962, the area was affected by radioactive fallout, with a comparatively high rate of cancer reported in the local population from the mid-1950s to the early 1980s.

Ninety-one of the 220 cast and crew who worked on *The Conqueror* subsequently developed cancer (41%), and 46 (21%) died from it, leading to suspicions that the film was cursed. Naturally, though, one has to wonder whether exposure to radioactive fallout played a role in some of the cases. It has been said that the number of cancers was in line with the average among adults at the time in the USA, and it may be that lifestyle factors account for some of the cases. For example, John Wayne reportedly attributed his stomach cancer to very heavy smoking. On the other hand, with many of those involved in the film, their cancer developed at a younger than average age.

### *Rosemary's Baby* (released in 1968)

Rosemary's Baby, a highly-rated horror film, was written and directed by Roman Polanski. Based on a successful 1967 novel, of the same title, by Ira Levin (1929-2007), it concerns a character called Rosemary Woodhouse (played by the actress Mia Farrow), who is impregnated by Satan and gives birth to his son.

Some of those who helped to create the film went on to experience misfortune.

Krzysztof Komeda (1931-69), who contributed music for the film and was a friend of Polanski's, was involved in a tragic accident in December 1968. During a drinking party, he was accidentally pushed off an escarpment by a writer called Marek Hłasko. Komeda incurred a cerebral haematoma and remained in a coma until his death in April 1969, at the age of 37. Hłasko himself died about two months later, aged 35, possibly of an accidental overdose of alcohol and sedative drugs.

William Castle (1914-77), the producer of *Rosemary's Baby*, was assailed by hate mail. In April 1969, he was troubled by kidney stones. In a delirious state in hospital, he reportedly had hallucinations related to the film. Although he recovered, he didn't produce another Hollywood hit.

On 9 August 1969, along with four others, Roman Polanski's heavily pregnant wife, actress Sharon Tate, was brutally murdered by members of a cult known as the Manson Family. Tate had sought the lead role in *Rosemary's Baby*, although Paramount, the film company, decided to cast Mia Farrow instead. Nevertheless, Tate appeared, uncredited, in the background in one of the scenes. According to a *Vanity Fair* article, Polanski last saw his wife in July 1969, and he noted in his autobiography a thought that he'd had at the time: that he would never see her again.[10] But Polanski's travails didn't end there. In 1977, he was charged with drugging and raping a girl of 13. In a plea bargain, he admitted to a lesser offence: having sex with a minor. But in 1978, he fled from the USA to Paris after learning that the judge intended to reject the plea deal and sentence him to prison rather than grant probation.

When she became involved in *Rosemary's Baby*, Mia Farrow was married to the singer and actor Frank Sinatra. Farrow had a planned role in his film *The Detective*, but as the shooting schedule for *Rosemary's Baby* stretched out, she had difficulty managing the schedules for both films. *Rosemary's Baby* won out, and Sinatra demanded that she choose between him and her film career. When she opted to complete *Rosemary's Baby*, he got his lawyer to deliver divorce papers to her at the film set.

As noted, Ira Levin was the author of the book on which *Rosemary's Baby* was based. He attracted criticism, with the Catholic Church condemning the film for mocking religious persons and practices. His first marriage ended in divorce in 1968. In a 1992 interview, he confessed to having mixed feelings about *Rosemary's Baby*. He seemed to regret that his work had helped to popularize irrational belief in the occult, witchcraft and Satanism. However, his book didn't send his career into a nosedive. On the contrary, subsequent novels were the basis for the acclaimed films *The Stepford Wives* (1975) and *The Boys from Brazil* (1978).

The Dakota, an apartment complex in New York City, featured in some of the filming for *Rosemary's Baby*. On the evening of 8 December 1980, the former Beatle John Lennon was shot and fatally wounded in the archway of the building. He and his wife, Yoko Ono, had an apartment there.

In terms of the distinction between Type I and Type II curses, there's also an alleged Type I aspect to this case. Nick Redfern, who hails from the UK but now lives in Texas, is a well-known researcher and author of books on anomalous phenomena. In his 2018 book *The Black Diary*, he cites incidents in which people have had strange experiences in connection with watching *Rosemary's Baby*, simply listening to the associated music, or after reading the novel on which the film was based (pp. 145-51). For example, an acupuncturist called Alison told him of a strange incident that occurred in California in 2010. It's reminiscent of the BEK cases mentioned in Chapter 6. She was lying in bed, watching the film at night in a motel room. There was a loud knock on the door, which alarmed her. After a few seconds, she tiptoed to the door. Looking through the spy-hole, she saw two boys in black hoodies and wearing black jeans. In a raised voice, one of them asked if they could use the phone. They were holding their heads low, meaning that Alison couldn't see their faces well. But moments later, she was able to, and she saw that their eyes were completely black. However, I imagine that many thousands of people have watched the film over the years, and most likely without experiencing any such creepy phenomena. The odd occasion when it happens will be much more likely to be reported than the many times when it doesn't.

On the night of 4/5th November 2016, Redfern watched his DVD version of *Rosemary's Baby*. Several hours later, around 8.30 a.m., he spotted what he deems to have been a Man in Black[11] walking along a path near his apartment block. He managed to take a photograph of the figure, which is included in his book. To me, though, the man doesn't look particularly sinister, and his attire doesn't appear to be noticeably black. For example, there's a light-coloured band around the hat that he's wearing.

### *The Exorcist* (released in 1973)

This horror film was produced by William Peter Blatty (1928-2017), who wrote the script, which is based on his 1971 novel of the same name. The movie was directed by William Friedkin (b. 1935) and centres on a 12-year-old girl called Regan MacNeil (played by Linda Blair, b. 1959) who is demonically possessed. The British film critic Mark Kermode has rated the film as his all-time favourite.

Max von Sydow (1929-2020) played a Catholic priest in the film. During its production, his grandfather died, as did the mother of Jason Miller (1939-2001), who played another Catholic priest. Linda Blair incurred a fracture in her spine during filming, which subsequently led to scoliosis and chronic pain; and one of her relatives died of a heart attack while the film was being made. Actress Ellen Burstyn (b. 1932), who played Regan's mother in the film, also had an accident, which left her on crutches for the remainder of the production. Things were also held up by a fire that destroyed most of the set. In her one-and-only film role, Greek-born Vasiliki Maliaros (1883-1973) played the mother of a Catholic priest in the film. She died in February 1973, reportedly of natural causes, before the film was released in late 1973. The Irish-born actor Jack MacGowran (1918-73), who played the character Burke Dennings, also died some months before the film came out. In his case, the cause of death was said to have been complications from influenza.

Because of the deaths and mishaps associated with it, *The Exorcist* acquired a reputation for being cursed. Despite mixed reviews, audiences flocked to see it. Some of them experienced marked physical or psychological reactions (e.g. fainting, vomiting, or soiling themselves); and a large number of people have reportedly died while watching it, although I'm not sure how significant this is (i.e. I don't know whether there are reliable comparative figures about people dying while watching films of different types). Many of the non-fatal reactions may be attributable to 'mass hysteria' or 'cinematic neurosis' rather than to a curse.

## *The Omen* (released in 1976)

This film, which has distinct parallels with *Rosemary's Baby*, has also acquired a reputation for being cursed. The movie concerns an American diplomat, Robert Thorn, who is played by Gregory Peck (1916-2003). Thorn's wife, Katherine, gives birth to a child in Italy. Robert is told that it was still-born, although it later transpires that the baby was murdered. At the hospital, a priest suggests to Thorn that he and his wife take a healthy newborn baby whose mother died in childbirth. Without telling Katherine, Robert agrees. The Thorns move to London, where Robert serves as the US Ambassador. Strange events and warnings from a priest eventually convince him that Damien, the child, is the Antichrist. Robert sets out to kill the boy, but he's shot dead by a policeman before he can do so.

According to Harvey Bernhard (1924-2014), who produced the film, the idea of a movie about the Antichrist came from his friend Bob Munger in 1973. Bernhard then hired screenwriter David Seltzer to write the screenplay.

I shan't attempt to cite all of the alleged incidents that occurred during or after the film's production. But problems began before it got underway. Gregory Peck's eldest son, Jonathan (1944-75), died of a self-inflicted gunshot wound in late June 1975. He was reportedly depressed as a result of overwork, a failed love affair, and a medical problem (arteriosclerosis). These factors may well account for the suicide. In other words, his tragic death may have had nothing to do with a supposed curse related to *The Omen*.

I have qualms about the historical accuracy of some aspects of this case, because sources differ regarding the details. For example, it's been said that while Gregory Peck was flying to London in September or October of 1975, the plane he was in was struck by lightning. Another story about him from around the time is that he cancelled a flight reservation and subsequently learned that the plane concerned had crashed, with everyone on board being killed. Did both of these things happen, or has there been some inventive myth-making?

It has been claimed that Mace Neufeld (b. 1928), the executive producer of the film, was flying to or from Los Angeles (sources differ as to the direction of the flight) when the plane was struck by lightning. David Seltzer, the screenwriter, is also said to have been in a plane that incurred a non-fatal lightning strike, although I don't know whether the story is true. And it's alleged that producer Harvey Bernhard came close to being struck by lightning during filming in Rome.

During the production, the director, Richard Donner (1930-2021), was reportedly staying at a British hotel (in London, I presume) that was bombed by the Provisional IRA (PIRA). But I don't know the name of the establishment, the date of the supposed incident, or whether the hotel really was attacked. Mace Neufeld is also alleged to have stayed at a hotel that was blown up by the PIRA. And he's said to have eaten, or planned to eat, in a London restaurant that met the same fate. In each case, he allegedly missed the explosion by just a few hours.

True or not, the stories don't end there. A plane that was nearly used for aerial filming crashed, with everyone on board being killed; and an animal trainer, who worked on-set, was supposedly killed by a tiger. For some involved in the film, there were allegedly problems when they went on to subsequent projects. For example, a stuntman called Alf Joint became involved in the war film *A Bridge Too Far* and was badly injured when something strange happened. He was supposed to jump from a roof onto an airbag, but he appeared to fall suddenly and awkwardly. After waking up in hospital, he told friends that he felt as if he'd been pushed.

## *Poltergeist* (released in 1982)

The film *Poltergeist* was released in 1982. The script was written by Steven Spielberg, Michael Grais, and Mark Victor, and based on a story by Spielberg. It features a suburban family whose home is invaded by ghosts, one of which eventually abducts their youngest daughter, Carol Anne Freeling, taking her to another realm.

The film is very loosely based on supposedly real events on Long Island, New York, in February and March 1958. It was a poltergeist case affecting a family called Hermann, and involved phenomena such as ornaments flying around and a heavy bookshelf toppling over. A police officer was nearly struck by a flying globe, and a British press photographer saw his flashbulbs lift off a table. Ministers from a range of faiths conducted rituals, but the disturbances persisted, to the consternation of the parents and their two children, aged 12 and 13. But then, for no apparent reason, the manifestations abruptly ceased. Shortly after, the Hermanns moved away. They thought the disturbances were related to a nearby ancient Native

American burial site. That's also a theme in the movie. Events occurring after its release earned it a reputation for being cursed.

Within weeks of the film's release, actress Dominique Dunn (1959-82), who played the part of Carol Anne's big sister, was strangled by her boyfriend. Brain-dead, she died five days later in hospital when her life support system was turned off. Lou Perryman (1941-2009), a small part actor in the film, was also the victim of lethal violence. He was killed at his home in Austin, Texas, by an axe-wielding ex-convict. But that was many years after he appeared in *Poltergeist*.

Child actress Heather O'Rourke (1975-88), who played Carol Anne in the film, is said to have died of shock caused by a blood infection, related to a birth defect that made a section of her lower intestine abnormally narrow. However, medical experts have expressed puzzlement, because she didn't have a prior history of symptoms of such a bowel defect.[12]

There were two further films in the *Poltergeist* series: *Poltergeist II* (released in 1986) and *Poltergeist III* (released in 1988). Subtitled 'The Other Side', *Poltergeist II* received mixed reviews, but was a financial success. Poltergeist III attracted negative reviews from critics and performed somewhat disappointingly at the box office.

Julian Beck (1925-85) played preacher Henry Kane in *Poltergeist II*. In late 1983, he was diagnosed with stomach cancer, and he died of it around the time the film was released. Will Sampson (1933-87) who played the role of a Native American shaman in *Poltergeist II*, died of post-operative kidney failure after undergoing a heart and lung transplant.

James Kahn (b. 1947) wrote a novelization to accompany Poltergeist II. He reported that just seconds after he wrote the words 'Lightning ripped open the sky', his work premises were struck by lightning and arcade games in a lounge began to play by themselves.

## *The Twilight Zone* (released in 1983)

The television series *The Twilight Zone* show was a mix of horror and science fiction. That's also true of the movie version. During filming of the latter, a low-flying helicopter spun out of control and crash-landed on top of the actor Vic Morrow (1929-82) and two child actors, six-year-old Renee Chen and seven-year-old Myca Dinh Le. All three were killed instantly. Because of this incident, it's been suggested that the film was cursed. Arguably, though, this was simply a tragic accident, not the outcome of a curse.

## *The Passion of Christ* (released in 2004)

This biblical drama was produced, co-written, and directed by Mel Gibson (b. 1956). It stars Jim Caviezel (b. 1968) as Jesus Christ. During filming of the Sermon on the Mount (at a remote location in Italy), Caviezel and the assistant director, Jan Michelini (b. 1979), were struck by lightning, although they weren't badly hurt. For Michelini, this was a second time: during filming at another location in Italy (Matera), he incurred light burns to his fingers when his umbrella was hit by lightning.[13]

On the basis of these lightning strikes, it has been suggested that the film is cursed. As noted, though, the people concerned weren't seriously injured. The film was financially successful and was nominated for Academy Awards.

## *The Dark Knight* (released in 2008)

This film, which was directed by Jonathan Nolan (b. 1976), is the second of a Batman trilogy. Although it did well at the box office, some of those who participated either died or suffered misfortune around the time, again giving rise to the speculative notion of a curse.

A special effects technician was killed in 2007 when a truck, carrying a camera platform, crashed into a tree near Chertsey, Surrey.

The Australian-born actor Heath Ledger (1979-2008), who played the Joker character in the film, died from an accidental overdose of prescription drugs at his Manhattan, New York, home in January 2008. That wasn't long after completion of the film, and about six months before its release.

In July 2008, Christian Bale (b. 1974), who played Batman in the film, was arrested in London following an alleged assault, although the Crown Prosecution Service eventually decided to take no further action.

Morgan Freeman (b. 1937), who played the role of Lucius Fox in the film, was involved in a motoring accident in August 2008. He and a passenger had to be cut free from the vehicle. Freeman incurred multiple injuries. The passenger subsequently sued Freeman for negligence, but the matter was eventually settled for an undisclosed amount.

## *The Stone: No Soul Unturned* (released in 2011)

Strictly speaking, the story about this British horror film is suggestive of a Type I curse rather than one of the Type II kind. But since we're talking about films, I'll include it here.

The screenplay was written by Philip Gardiner, who also directed it.[14] I tried watching it myself, but I found it lacking a coherent and comprehensible plot, with too much melodramatic 'mood music', and poor sound quality, although the latter may reflect a personal hearing problem rather than a defect in the soundtrack itself. Consequently, I gave up partway through. But from what I've read, the movie concerns a film crew who visit a supposedly haunted location, wanting to know the truth regarding life after death. Filming was conducted on location at centuries-old Annesley Hall in Nottinghamshire, which hasn't been lived in since 1997, when it was damaged by fire. As it happens, the Hall is reputedly haunted.

According to a recent article by Milton Grover, paranormal phenomena occurred at Annesley Hall during the making of *The Stone*.[15] The filming there apparently went on for seven consecutive days, but Grover doesn't say whether manifestations occurred on each of them. The phenomena began on the first day of the shoot, and reportedly during the first scene. Grover states that he was given exclusive access to accounts from Gardiner and several of the cast and crew. He may be referring to written or audio-recorded testimony rather than personal interviews. His wording doesn't make that clear. At any rate, he says that he has no doubt that the witnesses he cites were completely sincere, and that they were alarmed by what happened. The following are some examples.

Actor and musician Wes Dolan recounted that Gardiner's mobile phone rang during a scene, the call seemingly coming from an actress who was performing in it. However, the woman concerned didn't have her phone with her at the time. When it was checked later, it was found to be switched off. Dolan's own phone had been fully charged that morning, but it went flat within half an hour of his arrival on the set. And there were problems with most of the mobile phones belonging to the rest of the cast during shooting at the Hall.

In the case of Corjan Mol, who contributed music for the film, and who also seems to have acted in it, there was a phone-related incident at the hotel where he and fellow members of the cast and crew were staying. While he was having a shower, his phone came alive, playing a song at about a tenth of the normal speed. Consequently, the words were at a very low pitch, which he likened to the sort of voice used in horror films to portray a demon or someone possessed by one. However, it transpired that nothing seemed to be wrong with his phone.

The cellar of Annesley Hall once functioned as a mortuary. Actor Simon Dulay related that when he and actress Suzy Deakin went into it, the hairs on his neck stood up. He felt something touching him; and, at the same time, the ambient temperature seemed to drop rapidly. Deakin didn't notice that, although both she and Dulay had a distinct impression of being 'continually watched' in the cellar. (These are Grover's words, but I wonder whether he means 'continuously watched', the difference being that 'continually' implies something *intermittent*, while 'continuously' means *non-stop*.)

During filming of a 'stair fall', stuntman Nik Spencer was injured by a metal bracket that was lying on one of the steps. However, before the fall was filmed, the stairs were carefully checked, step-by-step, and swept from top to bottom, with some wooden splinters being removed. Furthermore, the fall during which Spencer was hurt was the third take, and no one else had been on the stairs around that time. Therefore, there's a mystery about how a metal bracket came to be there, and in a position to injure Spencer.

Grover asks whether this is another case of a film about the supernatural bringing about unintended paranormal effects. However, to the extent that Annesley Hall is, or was, haunted, it may be that the phenomena allegedly experienced by the cast and crew occurred simply because they were there, and not because they were making a film with an explicitly supernatural theme. On the other hand, if – as I suspect – there's a tricksterish intelligence behind phenomena of this type, it wouldn't surprise me if the supernatural theme of the film helped to catalyse paranormal manifestations at the site.

# CHAPTER 9

# REFLECTIONS AND SPECULATIONS

I've presented numerous cases in the preceding chapters, and along the way, I've included some commentary. In this chapter, I'll offer some further reflections and speculations. In doing so, I'll refer back to some of the cases I've cited.

## ARE SOME CURSES REAL?

In Chapter 1, I distinguished between *Type I* and *Type II* curses. With the first, the targeted person or group (e.g. a family) experiences disturbing phenomena of a distinctly paranormal character, whereas a Type II curse results in the target person or group experiencing a disproportionate amount of bad luck (accidents, deaths, etc.). However, as previously noted, some cases appear to involve both Type I and Type II elements.

Chapter 3 cites experimental evidence for the notion that people can exert paranormal physical effects and can influence the physiology of others. Regarding supposed Type I curses, the evidence suggests that some of them may indeed be real. Take, for example, Case 13 in Chapter 5, in which poltergeist phenomena reportedly occurred at the Edinburgh home of Alexander and Zeyla Seton after the latter purloined a bone from a burial tomb in Egypt. Of course, I can't be sure that Alexander Seton's account of what happened is accurate. But assuming that it is, it's noteworthy that the phenomena centred on the bone, or largely so. This suggests to me that the outbreak of poltergeist-type activity was related to the presence of the bone, and that its being taken from a burial tomb in Egypt may have unleashed a curse. However, a tricksterish and deceptive intelligence seems to be behind many paranormal manifestations. Therefore, it's conceivable that the phenomena had more to do with tensions in the Setons' marriage than anything else, and that the phenomena were deliberately orchestrated to give a false impression that irresponsible behaviour by Zeyla Seton had activated an ancient curse.

Regarding the 'Drummer of Tedworth' (Case 1, Chapter 4), the phenomena at the Mompessons' home had a persecutory flavour, and there's good reason to link the manifestations with the drummer, William Drury. For example, the auditory phenomena included drumming sounds. Therefore, the Mompessons may well have been the victims of a Type I curse.

The south London case (Case 2, Chapter 4) is also suggestive of a Type I curse. However, we can't be sure that the poltergeist phenomena at Carol Finn's home were related to her sister and brother-in-law's envy and resentment.

In the previous chapters, I've cited numerous examples of supposed Type II ('bad luck') curses. However, as I've pointed out, in most, if not all, of these stories, it's unclear whether a curse was really at work. Take, for example, the bad luck associated with the films mentioned in Chapter 8. Such productions may involve a large crew and cast, and the shooting may span many months. Consequently, it's perhaps only to be expected that deaths and accidents will occasionally occur, particularly if some of the production staff and cast, or their relatives, are middle-aged or elderly, and hence of an age when health problems, such as heart attacks and strokes, might occur. It's worth recalling, for example, that Vasiliki Maliaros was in her *late 80s* when she performed in *The Exorcist*.

But despite my misgivings about many supposed Type II cases, I'm not a total sceptic. For example, regarding the stories about black-eyed kids (BEKs) in Chapter 6, I find it intriguing that Beth (Case 7) reportedly experienced a string of upsets *very soon* after being visited by a couple of BEKs. Admittedly, that may have been purely coincidental, but the case gives pause for thought. On the other hand, the account is effectively anonymous, and it's seemingly uncorroborated, which limits its evidential value.

## ARE TYPE I AND TYPE II CURSES FUNDAMENTALLY DIFFERENT?

If some supposed Type II ('bad luck') curses are real, how might they work? One possibility is that they're simply stealthy versions of Type I curses. Imagine, for example, that Jill curses Dave, and that Dave then drops down dead with a heart attack. It could be that Jill (or some form of intelligence acting on her behalf) has interfered with Dave's physiology in a subtle, paranormal way, causing the heart attack. Alternatively, if Dave meets his end in a car crash, it could be that his alertness was manipulated, or that there was interference with the electrical or mechanical workings of his vehicle.

## WHAT ARE CURSES FOR?

If some curses are real, what purpose(s) do they serve? One possibility is that they're solely designed to inflict pain, misery, or death, in order to satisfy hostile or vengeful wishes (e.g. 'No one gets away with removing one of my bones from this tomb!'). Alternatively, they may be designed to have a deterrent function. If the stories about Tutankhamun's tomb (Case 9, Chapter 5) and other such sites are indicative of genuine curses being at work, the maledictions may have been designed to deter people from desecrating the sites or removing artefacts. By the same token, the Type I phenomena at Annesley Hall during the filming of *The Stone* (Chapter 8) may have been intended to deter people from being there. However, such a curse might backfire, by increasing the profile of a location, encouraging others to visit the site in the hope of experiencing paranormal thrills.

In some instances, a curse might be aimed at inducing people to take 'corrective' action, such as returning a stone to a place that it was taken from (see Cases 5 and 6, Chapter 5). Regarding Case 13 in Chapter 5, the poltergeist activity at the Setons' home may have been intended to get them to return the piece of bone to the burial tomb that it was taken from in Egypt. If so, it failed in that objective.

## HOW ARE CURSES EXECUTED?

In Chapter 1, I briefly alluded to the possibility that curses work in an automatic, mechanistic way. However, I think that's unlikely, because the enactment of a curse is something that seems to require intelligent direction and 'fine tuning'. For example, regarding the disturbances at the Setons' home in Edinburgh (Case 13, Chapter 5), the manifestations didn't occur just anywhere in the house, but usually in close proximity to the bone or fragments of bone. The implication is that whatever was behind the phenomena 'knew' where the item was.

Imagine a scenario. A man called Joe selects a spot where he wants to be buried after he has died. He then utters a curse to the effect that anyone who disturbs his grave will face retribution. Some years after Joe's death, the land concerned is bought by a property firm and turned into a car park. Joe's angry spirit then initiates a vendetta against the company. It takes the form of disruptive poltergeist activity at their head office. Now, in this case, Joe is both the *initiator* of the curse (the one who made it) and the *agent* (the one who carries it out). We might suppose that Joe's spirit uses ESP, to learn about the layout of the company's head office, and psychokinesis (PK), to produce disruptive physical effects there (overturning furniture, deleting computer files, breaking windows, etc.).

Now consider a somewhat different scenario. As before, Joe utters a curse, but this time it's not his discarnate spirit that carries it out, but a resourceful higher intelligence. Acting as the agent, the latter discerns the layout of the firm's head office via ESP, and uses PK to produce physical phenomena there.

But now consider a third possibility. Instead of being the direct cause of the phenomena at the company's premises, the higher intelligence forms a telepathic link with June, a secretary working there. But June herself is completely unaware of this. Given that she works at the head office, she knows the layout of the place well, and the higher intelligence can draw on this information via the telepathic link. Further, imagine that, without realizing it, June has latent psychokinetic powers, and that that's the reason why the higher intelligence has latched onto her. In effect, she has become a 'poltergeist focus', the immediate source of the disruptive phenomena. Again, though, she's not aware that she's being used in this way. Indeed, along with other staff at the company's office, she may find the disturbances decidedly frightening.

I'd suggest that the latter scenario, or something similar, is well worth considering in respect of Type I curses, and perhaps with some Type II cases as well. Indeed, it could be that some seemingly 'typical' poltergeist episodes are actually Type I curse cases. If so, we need to look beyond the 'focal person' in such cases and ask whether he or she is being *used* to pursue a paranormal vendetta.

## CAN COINCIDENCES BE MANUFACTURED?

Assuming that they're not merely chance events, how might we explain strange coincidences, such as Christopher O'Brien's experience in 1993 of seeing and hearing an old-fashioned helicopter the day after interviewing people who'd seen one some 13 years previously (Case 8, Chapter 2)? As O'Brien suggests, this may have been manufactured synchronicity.

One possibility is that he and the other witnesses that day experienced a collective hallucination induced by an intelligence that has the power to alter our perception. Alternatively, the posited intelligence may have produced a temporary materialization of a helicopter. In other words, the helicopter may have had a degree of physical reality, but only temporarily, rather like a 'spirit form' temporarily materializing at a séance with a physical medium. A third possibility is that the presumed intelligence was able to edit the memories of O'Brien and the other witnesses, leaving them with a compelling, but false, recollection of having seen and heard an old-fashioned helicopter.

## A HIGHER INTELLIGENCE

Throughout this chapter, and at previous points in the book, I've referred to the notion of paranormal phenomena being orchestrated by a *higher intelligence*. It's not an idea that will appeal to everyone. Indeed, I've seen this notion described as using one unknown to explain another. However, it makes sense when we take account of the significant degree of overlap that occurs between different types of paranormal phenomena. Take, for example, the colloquially named Skinwalker Ranch in north-eastern Utah (Kelleher & Knapp, 2005; McCue, 2019, pp. 199-213: Salisbury, 2010, pp. 214-44). Over the years, it has been the setting for a wide range of manifestations (UFO sightings, poltergeist-type activity, sightings of strange animals, etc.). Phenomena have been observed and recorded by reputable scientists, using state-of-the-art equipment. As in other cases, there's been a tricksterish aspect to the alleged manifestations. Some of the activity has had a hostile or persecutory flavour. For example, during the occupancy of a family called Sherman, between 1994 and 1996, there were cattle mutilations, and also an incident in which three ranch dogs died. Chasing a blue orb that seemed to be deliberately teasing them, the dogs followed it into a copse, where their remains were found the next day.

Given this overlap between supposedly different types of phenomena, it's only natural to conclude that they may share the same origin. The intelligence involved is evidently *very resourceful*, which justifies our describing it as a *higher* intelligence. However, it's not clear what its aims and objectives are.

In his book *UFOs & Nukes*, Robert Hastings (2017) adduces a wealth of testimony linking UFO sightings with the production, testing, storage, and deployment of nuclear weapons. Regarding ballistic missiles, he cites reports of these weapon systems malfunctioning when UFOs have been nearby. Usually, this has resulted in a temporary loss of launch capability. However, in a couple of instances – one in the 1960s and one in the early 1980s – *the launch sequence was activated*.

In respect of the first incident, Hastings' informant was David H. Schuur, who was a member of a Minuteman missile crew at Minot Air Force Base (MAFB), North Dakota, between December 1963 and November 1967 (*ibid.*, pp. 313-7). He was a first lieutenant during that time. The missile silos were located in a broad arc around MAFB, going, clockwise, from the south-east to the north. They were organized into alphabetically designated groups (known as 'flights'), ranging from 'Alpha', in the south-east, to 'Oscar', in the north. (Hastings provides a helpful outline map on page 569 of his book.) One night, probably in 1966 or 1967, while Schuur was on duty at the console in the Echo Launch Control Capsule, it was reported that security personnel at another capsule (probably Alpha's, to the east) were seeing a large, bright object hovering above some of their missile sites, moving from one missile to another. For a while (maybe an hour or so – Schuur couldn't be sure), the UFO passed over all the flights. While it was over Echo flight, there were anomalous readings from some of its missiles, and an 'inhibit' switch had to be activated, because 'Launch in Progress' indicators had come on!

The second incident allegedly occurred on 4 October 1982 at a Soviet intermediate-range ballistic missile base outside the Ukrainian village of Byelokoroviche (Hastings, *ibid.*, pp. 445-52). A huge UFO reportedly hovered over the base for hours, and an unspecified number of the missiles activated. The count-down proceeded for 15 seconds, but then it aborted. Although there were multiple witnesses, the UFO sighting was officially attributed to the dropping of flares during a military exercise. But that story may have been part of a cover-up.

In a more recent book, Robert Hastings notes that another UFO-related missile-activation event reportedly occurred in the USA in 1974, at Malmstrom Air Force Base in Montana (Hastings & Jacobs, 2019, pp. 72-3).

From such cases, we might infer that the intelligence behind the manifestations is concerned about the destructive effects, or potentially destructive effects, of nuclear weapons, and is perhaps hinting that it could intervene if we go too far. However, if that's the case, one has to wonder why it isn't showing its displeasure about overpopulation, deforestation, pollution, and other indications of humanity's poor stewardship of its planet.

# NOTES

## CHAPTER 1: INTRODUCTION

1. Connor Stringer, 'Woman terrorised by haunted painting found in Brighton', https://www.theargus.co.uk/news/19094523.woman-terrorised-haunted-painting-found-brighton/
2. Connor Stringer, 'Haunted painting found in Brighton could be "Voodoo Queen"', https://www.theargus.co.uk/news/19104257.haunted-paining-found-brighton-voodoo-queen/
3. Shantrelle P. Lewis, 'Marie Laveau, American Vodou queen', https://www.britannica.com/biography/Marie-Laveau
4. Joe Carter (23 October 2019), '9 Things You Should Know About Modern Satanism', https://www.thegospelcoalition.org/article/9-things-you-should-know-about-modern-satanism/
5. She was born Violet Mary Firth, but eventually took the name Dion Fortune. Waters (2019, p. 193) explains that the new name was based on the Firth family motto, *deo non fortuna*, meaning 'God, not luck'.
6. In German, both common nouns and proper nouns are spelt with an initial capital letter. Regarding its use in English, 'schadenfreude' is treated like other common nouns and spelt with a lower-case 's', unless it appears at the beginning of a sentence.

## CHAPTER 2: STRANGE COINCIDENCES

1. 'From the Archives: Chilling similarities of the murders of two young women – 157 years apart', https://www.birminghammail.co.uk/news/local-news/from-the-archives-chilling- similarities-of-the-murders-of-two-117606
2. 'John Lennon and the number nine', https://www.beatlesbible.com/features/john-lennon-number-nine/
3. Nataly Kelly (30 July 2013), 'Bad-luck numbers that scare off customers', https://hbr.org/2013/07/the-bad-luck-numbers-that-scar
4. https://aviation-safety.net/database/record.php?id=19630305-0
5. '15 November 1967', https://www.thisdayinaviation.com/15-november-1967/
6. 'Aircraft accident report', http://libraryonline.erau.edu/online-full-text/ntsb/aircraft-accident-reports/AAR72-34.pdf

7. Lauren Zumbach (23 May 2019), 'The legacy of Flight 191', https://graphics.chicagotribune.com/flight-191-anniversary/index.html
8. https://aviation-safety.net/database/record.php?id=19850802-0
9. 'Delta Air Lines Flight 191', https://en.wikipedia.org/wiki/Delta_Air_Lines_Flight_191
10. 'The Fallible Mind: The crash of Comair flight 5191', https://admiralcloudberg.medium.com/the-fallible-mind-the-crash-of-comair-flight-5191-cb80e005f73e
11. 'JetBlue plane in emergency landing after captain's apparent breakdown', https://www.theguardian.com/world/2012/mar/28/jetblue-captain-scre

## CHAPTER 3: THE PARANORMAL

1. Marilyn Schlitz & William Braud, 'Distant intentionality and healing: Assessing the evidence', http://marilynschlitz.com/wp-content/uploads/2013/01/Distant-Intentionality-and-Healing1997schlitz.pdf
2. Mario Varvoglis, 'Psychic (distant) healing', https://parapsych.org/articles/0/503/psychic_distant_healing.aspx?
3. Dean Radin, Marilyn Schlitz, and Christopher Baur, 'Distant healing intention therapies: An overview of the scientific evidence', https://www.ncbi.nlm.nih.gov/pmc/articles/PMC4654780/
4. Leonard Leibovici, 'Effects of remote, retroactive intercessory prayer on outcomes in patients with bloodstream infection: randomised controlled trial', https://www.bmj.com/content/323/7327/1450
5. Robert McLuhan, 'Miami Poltergeist', https://psi-encyclopedia.spr.ac.uk/articles/miami-poltergeist
6. John McKinlay, 'Noises in the night – and the suspect is a spirit', *Glasgow Herald*, January 17, 1975, p. 7. https://news.google.com/newspapers?nid=GGgVawPscysC&dat=19750117&printsec=frontpage&hl=en
7. Michael Tymn, 'Remembering Professor Archie Roy (1924-2012)'. http://whitecrowbooks.com/michaeltymn/entry/remembering_professor_archie_roy_1924_2012
8. 'Strange but True: Stocksbridge Bypass, Flitwick Manor & Muncaster Castle', https://www.youtube.com/watch?v=yiBWvPunLKU

9. Cindy Parmiter (1 July 2020), 'True ghostly encounters: Can home renovations wake the dead?', https://exemplore.com/paranormal/True-Ghost-Encounters-When-Home-Renovations-Wake-the-Dead

## CHAPTER 4: PARANORMAL VENDETTAS

1. Based on information from Mompesson, Glanvill noted that for several nights the house was 'beset with seven or eight in the shape of Men, who, as soon as a Gun was discharged, would shuffle away together into an Arbour' (quoted by Price, 1993, p. 55). However, this seems to have happened around the end of the disturbances. It's conceivable that these were people from the neighbourhood who had heard about the manifestations at the house and were drawn by curiosity.
2. There's controversy about the use of hypnotic regression in UFO research, because of the possibility of suggestion and imagination creating false or distorted memories.
3. Kevin Randle (7 July 2011), 'The crash of Philip J. Imbrogno', http://kevinrandle.blogspot.com/2011/07/crash-of-philip-j-imbrogno.html
4. 'Daniel Dunglas Home', https://psi-encyclopedia.spr.ac.uk/articles/daniel-dunglas-home
5. Erlendur Haraldsson, 'Indridi Indridason (medium)', https://psi-encyclopedia.spr.ac.uk/articles/indridi-indridason-medium

## CHAPTER 5: CURSED OBJECTS AND MATERIALS

1. The details at the beginning of the book about its date of publication are confusing. The year is given as both '2010' and 'MMXII'. The latter (meaning 2012) seems to be the correct year.
2. In an interview with Paul Screeton in 2012, Colin said that he thought the Heads were discovered in 1972. However, Screeton notes that Colin's sister Wendy had pinpointed the event as occurring when she was on honeymoon. On p. 226, he gives the date of that as 'April/May' in 1971 (presumably meaning that the honeymoon began in late April and continued into the early part of May). However, that may be slightly wrong, because on p. 23, he quotes from an item that Wendy posted to a message board of the magazine *Fortean Times*. She indicated, there, that her honeymoon in Scotland had been in 'late May/early June of 1971'.
3. The title page of the book gives the author's name as 'R. Macdonald Robertson', but I don't know whether 'Macdonald' was correctly a part of his surname or whether he used a middle name, for reasons of affectation,

to create a double-barrelled (and somewhat unwieldy) surname. But since that's the way it appears in his book, I'll refer to him as 'Macdonald Robertson' rather than 'Robertson'. He died in 1968.

4. The assertion that Sandwood Cottage is the most remote in Scotland is incorrect.

5. Searching on the Internet, I discovered that a Miss E. M. Van Horne of 5 Rothesay Place, Edinburgh, became a fellow of the Society of Antiquaries of Scotland in 1954. She may have been a daughter of the Mrs Van Horne mentioned by Halliday.

6. 'Accidental tourist returns "cursed" stone' (8 January 2000), http://news.bbc.co.uk/1/hi/scotland/595015.stm

7. Ian Lovett (14 May 2017), 'Curses! Hawaii can't get tourists to stop sending back lava', https://www.wsj.com/articles/curses-hawaii-cant-get-tourists-to-stop-sending-back-lava-1494784924

8. Carla Herreria Russo (updated 20 October 2016), 'The mysterious reason tourists keep mailing rocks back to Hawaii', https://www.huffpost.com/entry/peles-curse-lava-rocks-hawaii_n_5800337de4b05eff5582c5c7

9. 'SM *UB-65*', https://en.wikipedia.org/wiki/SM_UB-65

10. 'Iceman's discoverer dead in Alps', http://news.bbc.co.uk/1/hi/world/europe/3947461.stm

11. 'Konrad Spindler', https://de.wikipedia.org/wiki/Konrad_Spindler

12. Barbara McMahon (20 April 2005), 'Scientist seen as latest "victim" of Iceman', https://www.theguardian.com/science/2005/apr/20/science.italy

13. 'In memoriam: Thomas Harold Loy, 1942-2005', http://garethloy.com/TomLoy/In_Memoriam_Tom_Loy.html

14. James M. Deem, 'Curse of King Tut's Tomb: The facts', https://jamesmdeem.com/stories.mummy.kingtutcurse.html

15. Ann M. Cox (7 June 2003), 'The death of Lord Carnarvon', https://www.thelancet.com/journals/lancet/article/PIIS0140-6736(03)13576-3/fulltext

16. 'Marguerite Alibert', https://en.wikipedia.org/wiki/Marguerite_Alibert

17. David Castleton (31 March 2021), 'The Unlucky Mummy – Curse of the British Museum & sinker of the Titanic?' https://www.davidcastleton.net/unlucky-mummy-curse-british-museum-titanic-amen-ra-egyptian/

18. 'W. T. Stead', https://en.wikipedia.org/wiki/W._T._Stead

19. Holly Christodoulou (13 May 2020), 'Fright at the museum: Guards from British Museum report spooky goings on with ghostly footsteps and strange noises heard among the exhibits', https://www.thesun.co.uk/news/11608590/british-museum-haunted-exhibits/

20. Guy Walters (5 July 2020), 'A fright at the museum: The eerie happenings of the British Museum', https://www.you.co.uk/a-fright-at-the-museum-the-eerie-happenings-of-the-british-museum/

21. Stuart Minting (29 October 2014), '18th Century murderer's chair continues to captivate supernatural fans', https://www.thenorthernecho.co.uk/opinion/leader/11566417.18th-century-murderers-chair-continues-captivate-supernatural-fans/

22. I have some doubts about this story. If the rest of the woman's family was killed during the war, she couldn't have had a granddaughter, unless she was pregnant at the time of her alleged escape from the concentration camp, or unless she conceived sometime later. But if she died in 2001, at the age of 103, she would have already been in her forties when the Second World War began. Admittedly, though, some women do have babies when they're in their forties.

23. Kevin Mannis, 'Description of the dibbuk/dybbuk box for eBay', https://genius.com/Kevin-mannis-description-of-the-dibbuk-dybbuk-box-for-ebay-annotated

24. 'The dibbuk box', http://www.dibbukbox.com/

25. Carl 'The Disc' Fisher (13 July 2019), 'Horror movie review: Dybbuk Box: True Story of Chris Chambers (2019)', https://www.gbhbl.com/horror-movie-review-dybbuk-box-true-story-of-chris-chambers-2019/

26. Brian Dunning (19 August 2014), 'The haunted dybbuk box', https://skeptoid.com/episodes/4428

27. Kenny Biddle (14 January 2019), 'The dibbuk box', https://skepticalinquirer.org/exclusive/the-dibbuk-box/

28. 'Cursed Bone of Learmonth Gardens' (updated 17 December 2018), https://www.mysteriousbritain.co.uk/hauntings/cursed-bone-of-learmonth-gardens/

## CHAPTER 6: CURSED BY BLACK-EYED CHILDREN

1. I have misgivings about the expression 'urban legend', since there may be nothing particularly 'urban' about the settings referred to.
2. Brian Bethel (29 October 2017), 'Black eyed kid phenomenon', https://play.acast.com/s/somewhere-in-the-skies/brianbethel-blackeyedkidphenomenon
3. This chapter includes a photograph that I took on Cannock Chase, which is a 26-square-mile area of woodland and heath lying to the south-east of Stafford in the Midlands of England. However, I'm not claiming that any BEK encounters have occurred at the precise spot shown. It should be noted that many of the encounters mentioned in Lee Brickley's booklet supposedly occurred in nearby built-up areas and not on Cannock Chase itself.
4. Brickley's 47-page booklet presents 15 first-person accounts and one account supposedly written on behalf of the alleged witness. According to Brickley (p. 47), the 16 reports are just a fraction of those he has on file. But he states (p. 4) that the booklet contains some of the most interesting and terrifying accounts from 2013 to 2020. Two of the accounts end with 'Weird ay?' (which should be, 'Weird, eh?'). Therefore, it seems likely that at least two of the 16 reports were written by the same person. It may be that Brickley collected the reports (perhaps by a variety of means – email, text, word of mouth, etc.) and then wrote them up for his booklet in a style of his choosing. If so, much of the wording could be his, although the content may reflect what his informants told him. However, even if he has reproduced the content accurately, we can't be sure that the informants have told the truth. As in the case I've cited, the other 15 informants are anonymous, and their ages aren't given. Strangely, though, in all 16 accounts, specific times are given for the alleged events. For example, in one report (pp. 28-30), it's given as 3.12 a.m. I would have expected witnesses to be a bit vaguer about the time of their experiences (e.g. 'It happened around three in the morning').
5. Although many people spell it with a capital 'B', I prefer to use a lower-case 'b' for 'bigfoot', since the word is used as a common noun.

NOTES

## CHAPTER 7: FAMILY CURSES

1. Taysha Murtaugh (29 September 2017), 'The truth about Marilyn Monroe's alleged affair with John F. Kennedy', https://www.womansday.com/relationships/a60346/true-story-marilyn-monroe-john-f-kennedy-affair/

2. Katie Serena (updated 6 March 2020), 'The forgotten story of Rosemary Kennedy, who was lobotomized so that JFK could succeed', https://allthatsinteresting.com/rosemary-kennedy-lobotomy

3. Douglas Thompson (updated 3 July 2021), 'Did Bobby Kennedy murder Marilyn Monroe with poison? Shocking theory claims an ultra-secret LAPD file names JFK's brother as the killer – and a Hollywood actor watched it all unfold', https://www.womansday.com/relationships/a60346/true-story-marilyn-monroe-john-f-kennedy-affair/

4. Leora Arnowitz and Joey Garrison, 'Robert F. Kennedy's granddaughter, Saoirse Kennedy Hill, died of accidental overdose', https://eu.usatoday.com/story/entertainment/celebrities/2019/11/01/saoirse-kennedy-hill-died-of-accidental-overdose-at-22/4122556002/

5. Jeva Lange (29 January 2020), 'The dangers of private helicopters and planes', https://theweek.com/articles/892128/dangers-private-helicopters-planes

6. M. D. Seaton, 'Private flight is safer than ever (if you have a good pilot)', https://robbreport.com/motors/aviation/private-flight-safer-than-ever-good-pilot-2818709/

7. Chloe Foussianes (31 March 2019), 'The true story of Grace Kelly's death, and why rumors surrounding it have been so persistent', https://www.townandcountrymag.com/society/tradition/a26860987/grace-kelly-death-true-story/

## CHAPTER 8: CURSES IN THE MUSIC AND FILM INDUSTRIES

1. For the study, a 'famous musician' was defined as a solo artist, or any member of a band, that had had a No. 1 hit in the UK charts between 28 July 1956 (when the UK charts began) and 18 November 2007.

2. 'Is 27 really a dangerous age for famous musicians? A retrospective cohort study', https://www.bmj.com/press-releases/2011/12/20/27-really-dangerous-age-famous-musicians-retrospective-cohort-study

3. '27 Club myth', http://sciencenetlinks.com/science-news/science-updates/27-club-myth/

4. Other sources give different figures for the length of soundtrack that Page submitted to Anger.
5. 'The official website for Eddie & the Hot Rods', https://www.eddieandthehotrods.com/
6. 'Eddie and the Hot Rods: Barrie Masters' death drug-related', https://www.bbc.co.uk/news/uk-england-essex-53445878
7. Peter Watts, 'Jimmy Page, Aleister Crowley and the curse of Eddie And The Hot Rods', https://greatwen.com/2013/03/27/jimmy-page-aleister-crowley-and-the-curse-of-eddie-and-the-hot-rods/
8. 'Robert Johnson', https://en.wikipedia.org/wiki/Robert_Johnson
9. 'What really happened when Eric Clapton's 4-year-old son died in 1991', https://www.oversixty.com.au/entertainment/music/what-really-happened-when-eric-claptons-4-year-old-son-died-in-1991
10. Rosemary Counter (1 June 2017), 'The most cursed hit movie ever made', https://www.vanityfair.com/hollywood/2017/06/the-most-cursed-hit-movie-ever-made-rosemarys-baby
11. 'Men in Black' (MIB) and their female counterparts, 'Women in Black' (WIB), are creepy characters that visit, or otherwise show an interest in, people who've had UFO encounters or other odd experiences. As the name suggests, they're often attired in black or dark clothes; and they reportedly have a habit of travelling in new-looking, but old-fashioned, cars (such as Cadillacs), which may lack number plates. The MIB and WIB tend to be cryptic in what they say to people, and their general manner may be oddly gauche, as if they have only a limited understanding of how humans normally behave. For instance, an MIB might seem unsure about how to eat a commonly consumed food item. This could give the impression of an alien entity trying, with limited success, to pass itself off as human. However, there are other possibilities. For example, MIB and WIB may be government agents, sent out to intimidate UFO witnesses into keeping quiet about their experiences. But the various theories aren't all mutually exclusive, because there could be different types of MIB/WIB.
12. Lee Siegel (4 February 1988), 'Doctors: Unusual circumstances surrounded actress' death', https://apnews.com/article/355ac4e0f2b6bd8109f766de6ec0dfb8
13. 'Jesus actor struck by lightning' (updated 23 October 2003), http://news.bbc.co.uk/1/hi/entertainment/3209223.stm
14. 'The Stone', https://www.imdb.com/title/tt1786724/

15. Milton Grover (July 2021), 'Hex: The bizarre and alarming genesis of a film', *Phenomena Magazine*, Issue 147, pp. 28-31. (Issues of this magazine can be downloaded, free, via: https://www.phenomenamagazine.co.uk/about/)

# BIBLIOGRAPHY

Bainton, R. (2013). *The Mammoth Book of Unexplained Phenomena: Astonishing Anomalies, Unknown Dimensions, Panic and Paranoia.* London: Robinson.

Barrington, M. R. (2018). *JOTT: When things disappear…and come back or relocate…and why it really happens.* San Antonio, Texas: Anomalist Books.

Barrington, M. R. (2019). *Talking about Psychical Research: Thoughts on Life, Death, and the Nature of Reality.* White Crow Books.

Bem, D. J., Palmer, J. & Broughton, R. S. (2001). 'Updating the ganzfeld database: A victim of its own success?' *Journal of Parapsychology*, 65, pp. 207-18.

Brickley, L. (2021). *The Black Eyed Child of Cannock Chase.* Self-published.

Clelland, M. (2015). *The Messengers: Owls, Synchronicity and the UFO Abductee.* Richard Dolan Press.

Coleman, J. (2014). 'Let the right one in.' *Fortean Times*, 322, pp. 29-30.

Ferrol, S. (2014). 'Invasion of the black-eyed kids.' *Fortean Times*, 322, pp. 26-8; 31-2.

Fontana, D. (2005). *Is there an Afterlife?* Ropley, Hants.: O Books.

Fortune, D. (2001). *Psychic Self-Defense.* San Francisco: Weiser Books.

Fowler, R. E. (2004). *SynchroFile: Amazing Personal Encounters with Synchronicity and other Strange Phenomena.* New York: iUniverse.

Green, A. (1974). *Our Haunted Kingdom.* Glasgow: Fontana/Collins.

Halliday, R. (2010). *Edinburgh after Dark: Ghosts, Vampires and Witches of the Old Town.* Edinburgh: Black & White Publishing.

Hallowell, M. J. & Ritson, D. W. (2009). *The South Shields Poltergeist: One Family's Fight against an Invisible Intruder.* Stroud: The History Press.

Hastings, R. (2017). *UFOs & Nukes: Extraordinary Encounters at Nuclear Weapons Sites.* 2nd edition. Privately published.

Hastings, R. & Jacobs, B. (2019). *Confession: Our Hidden Alien Encounters Revealed.* Privately published.

Haxton, J. (2011). *The Dibbuk Box.* Missouri: Truman State University Press.

Holder, G. (2013). *Poltergeist over Scotland*. Brimscombe Port, Stroud: The History Press.

Hopkins, B. (1983). *Missing Time*. New York: Berkley Books. (First published in 1981.)

Imbrogno, P. (2008). *Interdimensional Universe: The New Science of UFOs, Paranormal Phenomena & Otherdimensional Beings*. Woodbury, Minnesota: Llewellyn Publications.

Jacobs, D. M. (1999). *The Threat: Revealing the Secret Alien Agenda*. New York: Fireside.

Kelleher, C. A. & Knapp, G. (2005). *Hunt for the Skinwalker: Science Confronts the Unexplained at a Remote Ranch in Utah*. New York: Paraview Pocket Books.

Konstam, A. (2005). *Ghost Ships: Tales of Abandoned, Doomed, and Haunted Vessels*. London: The Lyons Press.

Love, D. (2003). *Scottish Spectres*. Leicester: Ulverscroft.

McCloskey, K. (2020). *Unsolved Aviation Mysteries: Five Strange tales of Air and Sea*. Cheltenham: The History Press.

McCue, P. A. (2010). 'Renovation hauntings.' *Fortean Times*, 268, pp. 30-5.

McCue, P. A. (2012). *Zones of Strangeness: An Examination of Paranormal and UFO Hot Spots*. Bloomington, Indiana: AuthorHouse.

McCue, P. A. (2018). *Paranormal Encounters on Britain's Roads: Phantom Figures, UFOs and Missing Time*. Brimscombe Port, Stroud: The History Press.

McCue, P. A. (2019). *Britain's Paranormal Forests: Encounters in the Woods*. Cheltenham: The History Press.

McCue, P. A. (2021). 'The alleged haunting of Sandwood Bay: Fact or fiction?' *Anomaly: Journal of Research into the Paranormal*, 51, pp. 123-50.

Macdonald Robertson, R. (1995). *Selected Highland Folktales*. Isle of Colonsay: House of Lochar.

McHarg, J. H. (1977). 'A poltergeist case from Glasgow.' In J. D. Morris, W. G. Roll & R. L. Morris (eds), *Research in Parapsychology 1976*. Metuchen, New Jersey: Scarecrow Press, pp. 13-15.

Mack, J. E. (1995). *Abduction: Human Encounters with Aliens*. London: Pocket Books.

MacKenzie, A. (1997). *Adventures in Time: Encounters with the Past.* London: Athlone Press.

Nichols, A. & Roll, W. G. (1998). 'The Jacksonville water poltergeist: Electromagnetic and neuropsychological aspects.' *Proceedings of Presented Papers: The Parapsychological Association 41st Annual Convention,* pp. 97-107.

O'Brien, C. (2007). *Secrets of the Mysterious Valley.* Kempton, Illinois: Adventures Unlimited Press.

O'Brien, C. (2009). *Stalking the Tricksters: Shapeshifters, Skinwalkers, Dark Adepts and 2012.* Kempton, Illinois: Adventures Unlimited Press.

O'Brien, C. (2014). *Stalking the Herd: Unraveling the Cattle Mutilation Mystery.* Kempton, Illinois: Adventures Unlimited Press.

Ocker, J. W. (2020). *Cursed Objects: Strange but True Stories of the World's Most Infamous Items.* Philadephia: Quirk Books.

O'Keefe, C. (2021). 'The Battersea poltergeist.' *Fortean Times,* 404, pp. 24-36.

Owen, I. M. with Sparrow, M. (1976). *Conjuring up Philip: An Adventure in Psychokinesis.* New York: Harper & Row.

Powell, T. (2003). *The Locals: A Contemporary Investigation of the Bigfoot/Sasquatch Phenomenon.* Surrey, British Columbia: Hancock House.

Price, H. (1993). *Poltergeist: Tales of the Supernatural.* London: Bracken Books. (Originally published as *Poltergeist over England* by Country Life in 1945.)

Radin, D. (1997). *The Conscious Universe: The Scientific Truth of Psychic Phenomena.* New York: HarperCollins.

Radin, D. (2006). *Entangled Minds: Extrasensory Experiences in a Quantum Reality.* New York: Paraview Pocket Books.

Randles, J. (2001). *Time Storms: Amazing Evidence for Time Warps, Space Rifts and Time Travel.* London: Piatkus.

Redfern, N. (2018). *The Black Diary: M.I.B., Women in Black, Black-Eyed Children and Dangerous Books.* Lisa Hagan Books.

Ritson, D. W. (2020). *The South Shields Poltergeist: One Family's Fight against an Invisible Intruder.* Cheltenham: The History Press.

Ritson, D. W. & Hallowell, M. J. (2014). *Contagion: In the Shadow of the South Shields Poltergeist.* Limbury, Luton: Limbury Press.

Roll, W. G. & Persinger, M. A. (2001). 'Investigations of poltergeists and haunts: A review and interpretation.' In J. Houran and R. Lange (eds), *Hauntings and Poltergeists: Multidisciplinary Perspectives*. Jefferson, North Carolina: McFarland, pp. 123-63.

Roy, A. (1990). *A Sense of Something Strange: Investigations into the Paranormal*. Glasgow: Dog and Bone.

Salewicz, C. (2020). *Jimmy Page: The Definitive Biography*. London: HarperCollins.

Salisbury, F. B. (2010). *The Utah UFO Display: A Scientist Brings Reason and Logic to Over 400 UFO Sightings in Utah's Uintah Basin*. Springville, Utah: Bonneville Books.

Screeton, P. (2012). *Quest for the Hexham Heads*. Woolfardisworthy, Bideford: CFZ Press.

Sheldrake, R. (1999). *Dogs that Know when their Owners are Coming Home: And other Unexplained Powers of Animals*. London: Hutchinson.

Sinclair, P. (2016). *Truth-Proof: The Truth that leaves no Proof*. PBC Publishing.

Sinclair, P. (2017). *Truth-Proof 2: Beyond the Thinking Mind*. PBC Publishing.

Sinclair, P. (2019). *Truth-Proof 3: Bringing down the Light*. PBC Publishing.

Sinclair, P. (2020). *Night People: My truth, My Proof*. Truth Proof Publishing.

Sitwell, S. (1988). *Poltergeists: An Introduction and Examination followed by Chosen Instances*. New York: Dorset Press.

Underwood, P. (1980). *Gazetteer of Scottish Ghosts*. Glasgow: Fontana/Collins.

Underwood, P. (1994). *Nights in Haunted Houses*. Privately published.

Underwood, P. (2013). *Where the Ghosts Walk*. London: Souvenir Press.

Waters, T. (2020). *Cursed Britain: A History of Witchcraft and Black Magic in Modern Times*. New Haven and London: Yale University Press.

Watson, N. (2009). *The Alien Deception*. Privately published.

Weatherly, D. (2016). *Strange Intruders*. Nevada: Leprechaun Productions.

Weatherly, D. (2017). *The Black Eyed Children*. Nevada: Leprechaun Press.

# INDEX

| | |
|---|---|
| 27 Club, The | 139–40, 145 |
| | |
| Abilene, Texas | 113, 115–6 |
| Aho, Kalevi Ensio | 146 |
| Alibert, Marguerite | 101 |
| alien abduction | 65–7, 124 |
| alien greys | 114, 122, 124 |
| Amarillo, Texas | 28 |
| Amen-Ra | 103 |
| analytical psychology | 19 |
| Angell, Noah | 105 |
| Anger, Kenneth | 142–4 |
| Annesley Hall, Nottinghamshire | 155–6, 159 |
| Antichrist, The | 151 |
| Association for the Scientific Study of Anomalous Phenomena (ASSAP) | 87 |
| Athens, Greece | 132 |
| Atlanta, Georgia | 27 |
| Austin, Texas | 153 |
| Austria | 98–9 |
| Auty, Daniel | 106 |
| | |
| Bagans, Zak | 109 |
| Bainton, Roy | 20 |
| Bale, Christian | 154 |
| Balornock, Glasgow | 46–9 |
| Barnett, Adrian | 140 |
| Barrington, Mary Rose | 1, 36–7, 59–65, 73 |
| Battersea, London | 38 |

| | |
|---|---|
| Beatles, The | 3, 20, 141–2 |
| Beck, Julian | 153 |
| Bedfordshire, England | 49 |
| Beethoven, Ludwig van | 146 |
| Behe, George | 98 |
| Belgium | 93, 97, 130 |
| Bem, Daryl | 32 |
| Bénédite, Georges | 102 |
| Bernhard, Harvey | 151–2 |
| Bethel, Brian | 113–6, 123 |
| Bethell, Richard | 102 |
| Bey, Ali Kamel Fahmy | 101 |
| *Bible, The* | 12, 121 |
| Biddle, Kenny | 109–10 |
| bigfoot | 122–3, 170 (n. 5) |
| Birmingham, England | 20 |
| Black, Alasdair | 111 |
| black magic | 13–5 |
| black-eyed children | 4, 113–26, 149, 158 |
| black-eyed kids (BEKs) | See *black-eyed children* |
| Blair, Linda | 150 |
| Blatty, William Peter | 150 |
| Blyth, Northumberland | 85 |
| Boleskine House | 141 |
| Bolzano, Italy | 99–100 |
| Bonham, John | 140–4 |
| Boston, Massachusetts | 128–9 |
| Bowett, Adam | 107 |
| *Boys from Brazil, The* (film) | 149 |
| Brickley, Lee | 116, 170 (n. 3, n. 4) |
| Bridlington, E. Yorkshire | 65 |

# INDEX

| | |
|---|---|
| Bristol, England | 44 |
| British Museum, The | 103–6 |
| Broughton, Richard | 32 |
| Bruges, Belgium | 97 |
| Budge, Ernest Wallis | 104 |
| *Buffy the Vampire Slayer* (TV series) | 113 |
| Building renovations resulting in paranormal phenomena | 11, 49–53 |
| Burstyn, Ellen | 150 |
| Busby, Thomas | 106–7 |
| Byelokoroviche, Ukraine | 162–3 |
| Bywater, Hector Charles | 98 |
| | |
| Cairo, Egypt | 101–2 |
| California | 14, 26–7, 96, 99, 139, 149 |
| Cancer | 15, 18, 49, 102, 130–1, 147, 153 |
| Cannock, Staffordshire | 116–7 |
| Cannock Chase, Staffordshire | 116 |
| Cape Wrath, Scotland | 88 |
| Carter, Joe | 14 |
| Carter, Howard | 100–2 |
| Castle, William | 148 |
| Castleton, David | 103–4 |
| Castro, Fidel | 133 |
| Catholic Church | 14, 112, 135, 149–50 |
| cattle mutilations | 24, 161 |
| Caviezel, Jim | 154 |
| Chen, Renee | 153 |
| Chertsey, Surrey | 154 |
| Chesapeake Bay, Maryland | 132 |
| Chicago, Illinois | 27 |
| Church of Satan | 14 |

| | |
|---|---|
| clairvoyance | 30, 32 |
| Clapton, Conor | 146 |
| Clapton, Eric | 145–6 |
| Clava Cairns, near Inverness | 94–5 |
| Clelland, Mike | 25 |
| Cobain, Kurt | 139 |
| Coleman, Jenny | 113 |
| Colorado | 24, 131 |
| confirmation bias | 19, 24 |
| *Conqueror, The* (film) | 147 |
| Cox, Ann M. | 101 |
| Craigie, Des | 74, 80–1 |
| Cream (rock group) | 145–6 |
| Creed, William | 56–8 |
| 'Crossroads' (song) | 145–6 |
| Crowley, Aleister | 141–2, 144–5 |
| Cuban Missile Crisis | 129 |
| 'Curse of the Ninth' | 146 |
| curses – types of | 11–2 |
| cursing rituals | 10–2, 15, 55, 64–5, 81, 160 |
| | |
| Dakota, The (apartment building) | 21, 149 |
| Dallas, Texas | 5, 27, 129 |
| *Dark Knight, The* (film) | 154 |
| Deakin, Suzy | 156 |
| Deem, James | 102 |
| *Detective, The* (film) | 148 |
| Devon, England | 12 |
| Didier, Alexis | 73 |
| distant healing | 33–5 |
| djinn, The | 124 |

INDEX

| | |
|---|---|
| 'Do Anything You Wanna Do' (song) | 144–5 |
| Dodd family (Hexham) | 74–7, 79–80 |
| Dolan, Wes | 155 |
| Donner, Richard | 152 |
| Douglas, Graeme | 144 |
| Drummer of Tedworth | 4, 55–9, 158 |
| Drury, William | 56–9, 158 |
| Dulay, Simon | 156 |
| Dundee, Scotland | 22 |
| Dunn, Dominique | 153 |
| Dunning, Brian | 109 |
| 'Dybbuk Box', The | 107–10 |
| Dylan, Bob | 145 |
| | |
| Earnshaw, Tony | 107 |
| East Boston, Massachusetts | 128 |
| E. Sussex | 139 |
| E. Yorkshire | 65 |
| ectoplasm | 69–70 |
| Eddie & the Hot Rods | 144–5 |
| Edinburgh, Scotland | 78, 89–92, 110–2, 157, 159, 168 (n. 5) |
| Egypt | 12, 100–4, 110, 157, 159 |
| electronic voice phenomenon (EVP) | 39–40, 86 |
| Epstein, Brian | 20 |
| Erdington, Birmingham | 20 |
| Erskine, John (1st Earl of Mar) | 127–8 |
| evil eye | 12 |
| *Exorcist, The* (film) | 150, 158 |
| Extrasensory perception (ESP) | 22, 30–2, 69, 73, 160; see, also, *telepathy* |

| | |
|---|---|
| Farrow, Mia | 147–8 |
| Feachem, Richard | 78 |
| Federal Aviation Administration (FAA), USA | 28 |
| feeding off fear | 126 |
| Ferrol, Stuart | 113 |
| First World War | 97–8, 134 |
| Fleetwood Mac | 146 |
| Flight 191 | 1, 25–8 |
| Flitwick Manor, Bedfordshire | 49–50 |
| Florida | 27, 45–6 |
| Fontana, David | 69–70 |
| Fortune, Dion | 16–7, 165 (n. 5, Ch. 1) |
| Fowler, Raymond | 23–4 |
| France | 22, 101, 140, 148 |
| Freeman, Morgan | 154 |
| Freetown State Forest, Massachusetts | 117 |
| Friedkin, William | 150 |
| Freud, Sigmund | 19 |
| Fritz, Kurt | 99 |
| | |
| ganzfeld experiments | 31–2 |
| Gardiner, Philip | 155 |
| Genoa, Italy | 135 |
| Georgia, USA | 27 |
| Germany | 38, 97, 134 |
| *Ghost Adventures* (TV show) | 109 |
| Ghost Club, The | 44, 104 |
| Gibson, Mel | 154 |
| Glanvill, Joseph | 55–8 |
| Gornstein, Leslie | 109 |
| Goss, Michael | 98 |

| | |
|---|---|
| Gould, George Jay | 101 |
| Grais, Michael | 152 |
| Gray, Paul | 144–5 |
| Green, Andrew | 89 |
| Green, Peter | 145 |
| Grimaldi family | 5, 135–6 |
| Grover, Milton | 155–6 |
| *Grudge, The* (film) | 113 |
| | |
| Halliday, Ron | 1, 3–5, 91 |
| Hallowell, Michael | 1, 71, 81–7, 126 |
| Hallucinations | 38, 125, 148 |
| Hamburg, Germany | 97 |
| Haraldsson, Erlendur | 70 |
| Harding, Cooper | 106–7 |
| Hastie, Malcolm | 22 |
| Hastings, Robert | 162–3 |
| haunting and poltergeist cases | 4, 11–13, 29–30, 32, 35–53, 55–65, 70–1, 74–92, 97–8, 103–12, 155–9, 161 |
| Hawaii | 96–7 |
| Haxton, Jason | 108–10 |
| Hay, Cameron | 92 |
| Heary, Phil | 105 |
| Hendrix, Jimi | 139 |
| Henn, Rainer | 99 |
| Herbert, Aubrey | 101–2 |
| Herbert, George (Lord Carnarvon) | 100–2 |
| Herbert, Mervyn | 102 |
| Hermann family | 152–3 |
| Hexham Heads, The | 74–81 |
| Hlasko, Marek | 148 |

| | |
|---|---|
| Hodson, Frank | 80 |
| Holder, Geoff | 48 |
| Hollis, Ed | 144 |
| Holly, Buddy | 5, 140 |
| Holz, Rainer | 99 |
| Home, Daniel Dunglas | 70 |
| Hopkins, Budd | 65 |
| Hormones | 15 |
| Hunter, Jim | 42–3 |
| Hunter-Dorans, Bob | 94–5 |
| hypnotic regression | 65, 67, 167 (n. 2, Ch. 4) |
| Iceland | 70–1 |
| Imbrogno, Philip | 66–8 |
| immune system | 15, 101 |
| Indridason, Indridi | 68, 70–1 |
| Inverness, Scotland | 92–4 |
| Israel | 34 |
| Italy | 12, 98–100, 135, 151–2, 154 |
| Jacksonville, Florida | 45–6 |
| Jacobs, David | 65 |
| Jagger, Mick | 145 |
| Japan | 25, 106 |
| Jarrow, South Tyneside | 81–5 |
| jinn, The | 124 |
| Johnson, Robert | 145 |
| Joint, Alf | 152 |
| Jones, Brian | 5, 139, 145 |
| Jones, John Paul | 141–2 |
| Joplin, Janis | 139 |

| | |
|---|---|
| jott phenomena | 36–7 |
| Jung, Carl Gustav | 19 |
| | |
| Kahn, James | 153 |
| Kelleher, Colm | 161 |
| Kelly, Grace | 135–6 |
| Kennedy family | 4–5, 7, 127–33 |
| Kent | 13 |
| Knapp, George | 161 |
| Komeda, Krzysztof | 148 |
| Konstam, Angus | 97 |
| Kopechne, Mary Jo | 5, 128, 131 |
| | |
| Las Vegas, Nevada | 28, 109 |
| LaVey, Anton Szandor | 14 |
| Lawford, Christopher | 131 |
| Lawford, Peter | 130 |
| Le, Myca Dinh | 153–4 |
| Led Zeppelin | 140–5 |
| Ledger, Heath | 154 |
| Leibovici, Leonard | 34–5 |
| Lenin Vladimir | 134 |
| Lennon, John | 3, 20–1, 140, 149 |
| Laveau, Marie | 13 |
| Levin, Ira | 147, 149 |
| Lexington, Kentucky | 27 |
| Liverpool, England | 20–1 |
| Loch Ashie, Scotland | 92, 94 |
| Loch Duntelchaig, Scotland | 92–5 |
| Loch Ness, Scotland | 125, 141 |
| Loch Ness Monster | 125 |

| | |
|---|---|
| London, England | 1, 38–9, 56, 59–65, 71, 90, 102, 130, 139–40, 151–2, 154, 158 |
| Long Island, New York | 152–3 |
| Los Angeles, California | 27, 130, 151 |
| Louisiana | 13, 27 |
| Love, Dane | 90–1 |
| Loy, Tom | 99–100 |
| *Lucifer Rising* (film) | 142–3 |
| Ludgershall, Wiltshire | 56 |
| Lundy, John | 12 |
| | |
| McCloskey, Keith | 131 |
| McCue, Peter | 3–5, 39–43, 49–50, 87, 91, 114 |
| Macdonald Robertson, Ronald | 88–90 |
| Mace, Arthur | 102 |
| MacGowran, Jack | 150 |
| McHarg, James | 48 |
| Mack, John | 65 |
| MacKenzie, Andrew | 31 |
| Magee, Max | 47 |
| magnetic fields | 38, 46 |
| Maliaros, Vasiliki | 150, 158 |
| Malone, Post | 109 |
| Manhattan, New York City | 154 |
| Mannis, Kevin | 107–8, 110 |
| 'Manson Family' | 148 |
| Martin, Charlotte | 143 |
| Massachusetts | 23, 68, 117, 128 |
| Masters, Barrie | 144 |
| materialization | 68, 70, 124–5, 161 |
| Maxwell Park, Glasgow | 47–8 |
| mediums | 68–71, 161 |

| | |
|---|---|
| Men in Black (MIB) | 149–50, 172 (n. 11) |
| Miami, Florida | 45 |
| Michelini, Jan | 154 |
| Miller, Jason | 150 |
| Minot Air Force Base, N. Dakota | 162 |
| Minting, Stuart | 106–7 |
| missing time | 65–7 |
| Missouri, USA | 108, 123 |
| Mol, Corjan | 155–6 |
| Mompesson, John | 55–8 |
| Monaco | 5, 135 |
| Monroe, Marilyn | 129–30 |
| Moon, Keith | 140 |
| Morrison, Jim | 140 |
| Morrow, Vic | 153 |
| *Mortal Kombat* (film) | 115 |
| Moscow, Russia | 26, 133 |
| Munger, Bob | 151 |
| Murray, Thomas Douglas | 103–4 |
| | |
| National Security Agency, USA | 67 |
| National Transportation Safety Board (NTSB), USA | 26–7 |
| Nepal | 136–7 |
| Neufeld, Mace | 151–2 |
| Nevada, USA | 28, 109, 147 |
| New Mexico, USA | 24 |
| New Orleans | 13, 121 |
| New York City | 20–1, 117, 140, 146, 149, 154 |
| Nicholas II of Russia | 133–4 |
| Nichols, Andrew | 45–6 |
| Nietzke, Iosif | 108–9 |

| | |
|---|---|
| Nish, Davy | 94 |
| Nixon, Richard | 129 |
| Nolan, Jonathan | 154 |
| North Dakota, USA | 162 |
| North Tidworth, Wiltshire | 56 |
| North Yorkshire | 106–7 |
| Nottingham, England | 43–4 |
| Nottinghamshire | 43–4, 155–6 |
| nuclear weapons | 162–3 |
| | |
| object reading | 73 |
| O'Brien, Christopher | 24–5, 161 |
| Ocker, J. W. | 73, 98–9, 101–3, 106–7, 109 |
| oddjotts | 36–7 |
| O'Keefe, Ciaran | 38 |
| Oklahoma, USA | 132 |
| *Omen, The* (film) | 151–2 |
| Onassis, Alexander | 132 |
| Onassis, Aristotle | 132 |
| Onassis, Christina | 132 |
| Ono, Yoko | 149 |
| O'Rourke, Heather | 153 |
| Ossowiecki, Stefan | 73 |
| Oswald, Lee Harvey | 129 |
| Ötzi | 98–100, 102 |
| Owen, Iris | 35 |
| Owls | 25 |
| | |
| Page, Jimmy | 1, 141–5 |
| Palmer, John | 32 |
| Panufnik, Andrzej | 146 |
| parapsychology | 3–4, 29–30 |

| | |
|---|---|
| Paris, France | 140, 148 |
| Parmiter, Cindy | 50, 52 |
| *Passion of Christ, The* (film) | 154 |
| Peck, Gregory | 151 |
| Peck, Jonathan | 151 |
| Pele's Curse, Hawaii | 96–7 |
| Perryman, Lou | 153 |
| Philip Experiment | 35 |
| Plant, Robert | 141–3, 145 |
| Plant, Zarac | 143 |
| Plymouth Brethren | 141 |
| Polanski, Roman | 147–8 |
| Pollokshields, Glasgow | 47–8 |
| *Poltergeist* (film) | 152–3 |
| *Poltergeist II* (film) | 153 |
| *Poltergeist III* (film) | 153 |
| poltergeist contagion | 71 |
| poltergeist phenomena | See *haunting and poltergeist cases* |
| Portland, Oregon | 108 |
| *Possession, The* (film) | 109 |
| Powell, Thom | 123 |
| precognition | 30, 32 |
| Price, Harry | 1, 55–8 |
| Protestants | 14 |
| Provisional IRA | 152 |
| psi phenomena | 29; see, also, *clairvoyance, precognition, psychokinesis, retrocognition, telepathy,* |
| psychical research | 29–30, 47 |
| psychoanalysis | 19 |
| psychokinesis (PK) – defined | 30, 38 |
| psychometry | 73 |
| Puerto Rico | 26 |

| | |
|---|---|
| quantum physics | 32–3 |
| | |
| Radin, Dean | 31–2 |
| Randles, Jenny | 23, 28 |
| Rasputin, Grigori | 134 |
| recurrent spontaneous psychokinesis (RSPK) | 38 |
| Redfern, Nick | 149–50 |
| Reid, Archibald Douglas | 102 |
| retrocognition | 30–1 |
| Reykjavik, Iceland | 70 |
| Ritson, Darren | 1, 71, 81, 83–5, 126 |
| Robinson, Jeffrey | 135 |
| Robson, Douglas | 80 |
| Robson family (Hexham) | 74–8 |
| Roll, William | 45 |
| Romanov dynasty | 5, 133–4 |
| *Rosemary's Baby* (film) | 147–51 |
| Ross, Anne | 74, 78–80 |
| Roy, Archie | 47–8 |
| Ruby, Jack | 129 |
| Russia | 5, 133–4 |
| | |
| St George, Utah | 147 |
| Salewicz, Chris | 1, 142–3 |
| Salisbury, Frank | 161 |
| Sampson, Will | 153 |
| San Antonio, Texas | 119 |
| San Luis Valley, USA | 24–5 |
| Sandwood Bay, Scotland | 87–9 |
| Sandwood Cottage | 88–91 |
| Satan | 14, 147–8 |

| | |
|---|---|
| Satanism | 14, 149 |
| Schuur, David | 162 |
| Screeton, Paul | 74–80 |
| Seattle, Washington | 139 |
| Seltzer, David | 151 |
| serial killers | 83–4 |
| Seton, Alexander Hay | 110–2, 157, 159 |
| Seton, Zeyla | 110–2, 157, 159 |
| Sheldrake, Rupert | 30 |
| Simon, Erika | 98–9 |
| Simon, Helmut | 98–100 |
| Sinatra, Frank | 148 |
| Sinclair, Paul | 65–6 |
| Sirhan Sirhan | 130 |
| Sitwell, Sacheverell | 55 |
| Skakel, Ann | 132 |
| Skakel, George | 132 |
| Skakel, George Jr | 132 |
| Skinwalker Ranch, Utah | 161 |
| sleep paralysis | 82 |
| Society for Psychical Research (SPR) | 36, 61–3 |
| South Shields, South Tyneside | 71, 81 |
| South Tyrol, Italy | 98–9 |
| Southampton, Hampshire | 74, 79–80, 104 |
| Soviet Union | 26, 129, 162 |
| Spain | 108 |
| Sparrow, Margaret | 35 |
| Spencer, Nik | 156 |
| Spielberg, Steven | 152 |
| Spindler, Konrad | 99 |
| Stack, Lee | 102 |

| | |
|---|---|
| Staffordshire, England | 116–7 |
| Stead, William Thomas | 104 |
| *Stepford Wives, The* (film) | 149 |
| *Stone: No Soul Unturned, The* (film) | 155–6 |
| Suffolk, England | 31 |
| Sutherland, Scotland | 87–91 |
| synchronicity | 19–28, 161 |
| | |
| Tate, Sharon | 148 |
| Telepathy | 3–4, 30, 32–5 |
| Texas, USA | 5, 27–8, 113, 119–20, 129, 149, 153 |
| Thelema | 141–2 |
| thought-forms | 125 |
| *Titanic, The* (ship) | 104–5 |
| tulpas | 125 |
| Turkmenistan | 26 |
| Tutankhamun | 100–3 |
| *Twilight Zone, The* (film) | 153–4 |
| | |
| *UB-65* (submarine) | 97–8 |
| Underwood, Peter | 43–4, 89–90, 104 |
| unidentified flying objects (UFOs) | 4, 23, 65–8, 122, 161–3 |
| 'Unlucky Mummy', The | 103–5 |
| USSR – see *Soviet Union* | |
| Utah, USA | 147, 161 |
| | |
| Van Horne family | 90–1 |
| Varvoglis, Mario | 1, 33–4 |
| Vasquez, Julio | 45 |
| Victor, Mark | 152 |
| Virginia, USA | 50–3 |

| | |
|---|---|
| von Sydow, Max | 150 |
| Voodoo | 13 |
| | |
| Wales | 78–80 |
| Warnecke, Dieter | 99 |
| Waters, Thomas | 12, 16–7 |
| Watson, Nigel | 65 |
| Wayne, John | 147 |
| Weatherly, David | 12, 113–4, 116–24, 126 |
| white magic | 13–4 |
| Who, The | 140 |
| Wiltshire | 55–9 |
| Winehouse, Amy | 5, 140 |
| Winlock, Herbert E. | 102 |
| witchcraft | 7, 9–10, 13–14, 16–7, 58, 135, 149 |
| Women in Black (WIB) | 172 (n. 11) |
| | |
| *X-Files, The* (TV series) | 113 |
| | |
| Yardbirds, The | 141 |
| Yekaterinburg, Russia | 134 |

www.ingramcontent.com/pod-product-compliance
Lightning Source LLC
Chambersburg PA
CBHW060524100426
42743CB00009B/1421